# Seasons of Sisterhood

# Advance Praise

"I endorse this beautiful book and spirited reflection about life in Cameroon with great joy. I have known Mrs. Ambrosia Mondoa and her family for over 20 years. Mrs. Mondoa was instrumental in hosting +Christian Cardinal Tumi at my parish back in 2012. I even had the blessing of travelling with Mrs. Mondoa to Cameroon in 2017 for an amazing two-week journey.

Mrs. Mondoa is actively involved in sharing her culture and experience with others. Bringing people to respect and enjoy the culture of others is a task and ministry that she does very well. This is a gift that she offers to all she meets. Meeting her is exciting because Mrs. Mondoa enjoys and celebrates life, culture, and faith."

—**Vy. Rev. Roger F. DiBuo**, V.F., STL, Pastor, St. Elizabeth Catholic Church, Wilmington, DE

"*Seasons of Sisterhood* reads like a spiritual adventure into the sacred courts through the myriad corridors and tunnels of our mysterious origins and who we are. This book takes you through an emotional roller coaster journey into self-discovery, at the end of which you are "whammied" by a realization! "This is my story, which I certainly did not write." Here, in *Seasons of Sisterhood*, dreams do indeed become reality! My identical garden replicated but with different names for what I know."

—**Rev Pamela Martin**, Pastoral Counsellor & retired educator

"From page one, the authors plunge readers into a rich tapestry of family, friends, strangers, culture, history, and more. Our travelling sisterhood sojourns through Cameroon and learns about themselves and each other. This volume is an inspiring read for many audiences and has takeaways for all.

The vivid images and lush language create a realistic reading experience that evokes all five senses. Through a beautifully described Cameroonian backdrop, coupled with the triumphs and tribulations of family and friendship, this book beautifully conveys the journey of discovery of country and self."

—**Jack Bradley**, Ed.D.


"*Seasons of Sisterhood* can aptly be described as a Season of Music, discovery, and Reconnection. The book beautifully recounts the experiences of five women from the African diaspora and American backgrounds who undertook a 28-day trip of adventure, music, and discovery for some and reconnection with ancestral land for others.

For the diaspora, reconnect with your roots. Reminisce and discover gems that are still waiting to be discovered. For those who have never ventured out of their comfort zones, there is more out there to expand your mind. *Seasons of Sisterhood* is a great source to whet your appetite and, at the same time, prepare you for exciting discovery and growth. Who knows, you may create your own lifetime bonds with your own Mr Gilbert."

—**Dr. John Ajongwen**, World Financial Group & Merck Co Inc


"If you are thinking of travelling to Cameroon, or even travelling at all, and have questioned whether the trip is worth it, *Seasons of Sisterhood* is a resource for experiencing a life-changing trip right in your home. *Seasons of Sisterhood* did everything it was supposed to do. It entertained, educated, illustrated, and invited its readers to experience the sights and scenes within Cameroon. The captivating story is told from the lens of five women - from both African and

American backgrounds who go on a month-long adventure to Cameroon in hopes of reconnecting with the lands of their ancestors and exploring new cultures."

**Ngwa Numfor,** MA, Correspondent for The Athletic & The New York Times; author of *Muses of a Melanin Man Volume 1: Break Free From Conventional Thought* (2022).

"I wholeheartedly endorse and recommend this book for everyone's reading. These ladies' accounts of their trip to Cameroon, their infectious bonding despite their cultural and age differences, and the descriptive power of their narratives have made me feel compelled to travel to Cameroon again and visit the places they visited. I lived in Cameroon with my parents from age nine and schooled in East and West Cameroon for nine and a half years. I have gone back at different times to film in Cameroon, in English and French, but I've never experienced Cameroon like they did!

It's an amazing and exciting book to read, even for those who live in Cameroon, not to mention those who have never been there and, of course, Cameroonians in the Diaspora.

Well done ladies! Don't stop writing! You've got a lot more to offer the world through your writing. I can't wait to purchase and own my copy!"

—**Zack Orji,** Actor & Filmmaker.

"...The interest of these ladies of different backgrounds and cultures in visiting Cameroon is reassuring to me, and they will come again and motivate others to visit Cameroon. They are interested in sharing their stories and experiences with others, a sign that their narratives are not just about what they saw or heard but also what they felt in their hearts."

—**Dr. Edmund O Agbor,** Retired Surgeon, Catholic Diocese of Buea, South West Region, Cameroon

# Seasons *of* Sisterhood

*The Magic of our Journey to Cameroon*

Matanda Wawa Mondoa
Kanla Rachel Ngeh
Sarah Emily Craster
Christina Margaret Lisk
Ambrosia Kweh Mondoa

**SPEARS BOOKS**
Denver, Colorado

Spears Books
An Imprint of Spears Media Press LLC
7830 W. Alameda Ave, Suite 103-247
Denver, CO 80226
United States of America

First Published in the United States of America in 2024 by Spears Books
www.spearsbooks.org
info@spearsmedia.com
Information on this title: www.spearsbooks.org/seasons-of-sisterhood
© 2024 Matanda W. Mondoa, Kanla Ngeh, Sarah E. Craster, Christina M. Lisk, Ambrosia Kweh-Mondoa
All rights reserved.

No part of this publication may be reproduced, distributed, or transmitted in any form or by any means, including photocopying, recording, or other electronic or mechanical methods, without the prior written permission of the publisher, except in the case of brief quotations embodied in critical reviews and certain other noncommercial uses permitted by copyright law. For permission requests, write to the publisher, addressed "Attention: Permissions Coordinator," at the above address.

ISBN: 9781957296395 (Paperback)
Also available in Kindle format & Google Books

Spears Media Press has no responsibility for the persistence or accuracy of urls for external or third-party internet websites referred to in this publication, and does not guarantee that any content on such websites is, or will remain, accurate or appropriate.

Designed and typeset by Spears Media Press LLC
Edited by PATAMAE Research and Editing Consultancy

To all our family members and in gratitude for the unconditional love and care we received from two illustrious godsends, H.E. Philemon Yang and His Eminence Christian Cardinal Tumi.

# Contents

| | |
|---|---|
| *Acknowledgement* | xi |
| INTRODUCTION | xiii |
| CHAPTER ONE: The Troubadours<br>**Auntie Rachel** | 1 |
| CHAPTER TWO: Ancestral Homecoming<br>**Matanda** | 30 |
| CHAPTER THREE: The Grand Tour<br>**Sarah** | 70 |
| CHAPTER FOUR: Dad's Wish Fulfilled<br>**Auntie** | 115 |
| CHAPTER FIVE: On Sisterhood and Storytelling<br>**Christina** | 135 |
| *About the Authors* | 148 |

## ACKNOWLEDGEMENT

The warm home welcome and the endless support and sacrifices of our family members gave us the best of fun and a memorable vacation. Our friends in or behind the scenes sacrificed greatly for the homeliness we all felt. And there are others whom we cannot easily put in one category but without whom this book would never have come to light. To all, thank you.

# INTRODUCTION

The reality of being born an African Princess in the United States is intriguing. Your mind starts spinning around that moment when, as it were, you would come into your own and physically bond with your heritage in its pristine physicality. Silently in the depths of your heart, loud thoughts question when that moment will come.

It was in the background of this prescient knowledge that, prompted by questions posed after Auntie and I returned from a trip to Cameroon in 2015-2016, Auntie decided that the time was ripe and that it mattered for Matanda to visit her ageing Grandparents in Ndop to tap into the rich African heritage of her roots first-hand.

That decision spiralled into an unstoppable drive of curiosity, excitement, and a sense of adventure, desiring discovery of the land called Cameroon. Also called Africa in miniature, Cameroon held Matanda's roots, particularly ensconced in the town of Ndop, some twenty-five miles from Bamenda in the North West Region of Cameroon. From there came Matanda's Mum (Auntie), who extended the joyfully appreciated invitations to Matanda's two friends, Christina and Sarah. They constituted a team of troubadours along with Matanda throughout the journey. Their musical outings during the entire trip were a gratitude motif that upgraded the sense of pleasure and leisure during the journey. Auntie and I punctuated the young trio to form the travelling family, bonded by kindred affection, a sisterhood of shared experiences, particularly in those seasons of adventurous leisure that constitute this book's blueprint.

    They were seasons of sisterhood, but each experience was felt, emphasised, or expressed differently, especially because of the diversity of quietly nuanced differences in our cultural backgrounds. Here then, is an anthology of discovery seen through lenses differently curved. Naturally, overlapping recalls are a marker of different dreams coming true. The real time was the Summer of 2017, and the pointed trip was to Grandpa and Grandma for Matanda. But what the rest of us shared was felt to be worth recording as it raised a sense of fulfilment and gratitude that lives on in our hearts and should be expressed.

Kanla Rachel Ngeh

CHAPTER ONE

## Auntie Rachel

# THE TROUBADOURS

It was a rollercoaster trip of twenty-four days from June 20th to August 8th, 2016. It may well have been a trip around the world, twenty-four spent in Cameroon, less two days from and back to Newark, Delaware, on the East Coast of the United States. The tang was in the novelty of firsts, particularly for Matanda. It was her first trip to Cameroon, to Africa. This exhilarating experience of the journey with her friends, Christina and Sarah, was in anticipation, a knockout. Matanda's Mum and I (Auntie Rachel) were also part of the crew. Chaperoning was not exactly our role, for we were more enablers, and facilitators who opened the right doors and ensured the proper tone, especially as cultural, commercial and interactive manners tended to be rather sophisticated, requiring more tried hands and minds. We took the Brussels Airways commercial airline, with transit in Europe, before landing in Cameroon. We arrived in Yaoundé at Nsimalen International Airport, which would also be our exit point.

\*\*\*

**Airborne to Plenitude**

On the eve of the travel day, we had Holy Mass. It was a way of harnessing spiritual blessings, part of preparations for the trip. The next was a family meal, dinner at home; as a family, we enjoyed each other's company. Anticipation was in the air, rather like the last few days of Advent, anticipating the heightened joys of Christmas and then New Year.

The journey to the airport in Newark, NJ, was by Delaware Express Bus. Dr Emil Mondoa accompanied us on the two-and-a-half-hour ride in smooth traffic all along. The sun blessed the skies, which were brightly cloudy but moderately warm—beautiful weather. Our hearts warmed with it and with expectancy.

With the flow of the splendid weather, each of us dressed colourfully, albeit in classic trim, to celebrate the start of this journey. It was a feast or celebration long drawn out, as it were. We shared picture moments upon arriving at the airport before checking in our luggage and going through the boarding process. Of course, being a five-member crew dragged out the process somewhat, but we eventually were through. On board, we sat close to each other to easily interact directly. For example, I could walk only a few seats ahead of me to converse with the rest of the team. We settled happily in our seats and buckled up at the command of the flight captain, readying for flight take-off, which was without any noticeable incident.

For me, the timing of the trip had further significance because 20th July dawned into the 21st, my birthday— a birthday airborne on Brussels airline en route to Cameroon. By itself, that was a special treat, a day of gratitude, and I thanked God for his abundant graces upon my life. Each member of the crew had beautiful, heart-warming birthday wishes for me. We hugged, laughed, and smiled heartily. It was a moment so special in context that it was stamped in my memory.

Dawn came with a beautiful day outside, seen from my window seat as our plane smoothly ploughed the rolling batches and bales of clouds with little turbulence—shafts of sunrays shot through clean clouds, white and deeply bright blue. The journey was good and the going good. The hostesses competed in beating their own best by plane services that were consistently appreciable throughout the trip.

At the two-hour layover at Brussels airport in Belgium, we explored the shops and restaurants for food and gifts for family and friends. We feted and then settled down close to our boarding terminal to Cameroon. It is evidence of the pleasurable smoothness of the journey that, before we knew it, the plane was flying at a low level and providing the opportunity of a lifetime view of the beautiful city of Yaoundé. The wavy spread of its topography, relief, and city structure; the multiply shaded lights, the web of roads, nests of houses and plenitude of green farmlands of arresting crops held us spellbound.

With assertive slowness, the plane was making its way to landing, exerting less and less turbulence until it came to a complete stop. A safe landing it was, following a successful journey that had taken us to the Yaoundé Nsimalen International Airport.

What followed was a brisk routine as we disembarked through the presidential lounge, took to the luggage terminal for our luggage and went out through the checkout doors. Warm, I should say *hot*, family welcome greeted us outside. Our luggage fitted into two cars, and off we drove to the rental residence. Dinner at home was perfect - natural fresh food, processed in excellent cuisine, thanks to our sisterly friend, Balky, as well as Louis and his wife.

Matanda, Sarah and Christina thrilled us with music as

soothing socialisation and relaxation swelled the atmosphere. They had it that the natural beauty and experience of novelty would not be had for nothing. This no-free-bread mentality typifies us in the West, where we miss out on the stark fact that some situations and experiences are unqualified, unquantified and non-commodifiable. It was not until shortly after midnight that we retired to bed, and the day as recorded in my diary, was July 21st, 2016, Yaoundé - Cameroon.

*** 

If the 21st of July 2016 was beautifully fruitful, the following day was more eventful. The eventful start came in the later part of the morning when at a fee of 4000 FCFA for citizens and 10,000 FCFA for foreigners, we were ushered into the national museum. It was the converted palace of Cameroon's first President, Ahmadou Ahidjo. In-packed are representations from the ten regions of Cameroon, its people, cultural diversity, political and economic life.

For a start, we had the restriction - no technological gadget was let in. This heightened the mystique and the sacred preserve of the sanctum of artefacts. You were not even allowed to take in any personal item. So, as it were, you were led into the holy of holies to contemplate its beauty undistracted by anything foreign to it. And indeed, your concentration rose to ecstatic levels in there, everything you carried having been surrendered into a locked cabinet. A uniquely arresting sculpture of a queen adorned the main entrance to the museum.

It was important for Matanda, Christina and Sarah to see and appreciate everything for themselves and for what they were. But the excitement was in the air for all of us. We all looked forward to it. This, even though I was coming in with some pre-knowledge of the museum, having been there before. It was a maze of endless rooms of troughs, and it was not long before we realised that it would be impossible to tour all the rooms (about 30) in the two hours we had.

The rooms we toured nonetheless imparted meaningful experiences to us all. There were things I had learned about in primary (elementary) and secondary (middle) school studies. But there was a world of difference between the theoretical information of the classroom and the sensual, visual, and tactile exposure we were now offered. In real-time and concrete place, we encountered the artefacts, the professional arts and crafts work, and photo archives, unravelling an excellent narrative of a country fondly referred to as 'Africa in miniature.' It was a history of blood and beauty, of colonisation and independence etched in photo archives.

There, one discovered that the ordinary can be a milestone of history. Thus, the otherwise ordinary seat of a leader took on an iconic status, being the chair of the former Prime Minister of Anglophone Cameroon, Mr John Ngu Foncha. From its gruff use as a mere seat, it was now on high display. Likewise, the saxophone, a musical instrument of Cameroon's super-talented musician, Manu Dibango, was showcased to enshrine national pride. Pictures and artefacts of the pygmies, the actual original inhabitants of most of the southern part of Cameroon, caught my attention. Connecting the past with the present is that the pygmies still inhabit their natural environment, and their forest habitats are protected by the Cameroon government. Naturalists with distinct cultural and belief systems, the pygmy is phenomenal and the narrative on that unique group of people is well preserved in the museum, easily accessible to visitors.

The pygmy strand is only a scratch on the complex ethnicity of the country which, in the first place, is a divide of two colonial heritages - French Cameroon and English Cameroon, with attendant two, sometimes diametrically different cultures. The knottiness is compounded by the fact that under this overall dichotomy, it is a nexus of some 250 ethnic groups and languages. The official languages are French and English, although Pidgin English and Hausa are widely spoken along with the segments of ethnic languages and dialects. The French/English official bilingualism makes Cameroon one of the two bilingual countries in the world, the other being Canada.

The exhibitions in the museum echoed this national complexity of the different cultures, people, variant geographic scenery, and touristic sites. Overwhelmingly powerful and intellectually reinforcing was the experience. Mine had been predominantly experiences of an English-speaking Cameroonian, and resonating artefacts of this background stared unblinkingly at me. Different forms of crafts, textiles, articles, artefacts and photos spoke to my primal senses. It was exciting and stirred stunning feelings of wonder as I instantly connected the experience with both the writings I had read and the unravelled reality of *realia* right before my eyes.

The museum experience would boost the reminiscences of the trip we were to take to the North West Region. As the saying goes, there was as much in the process as in the destination. Transitions on the journey up were more of splicing from warmer to more temperate climates, from the tropical density of trees to the sparse and then to savannah rows and meadows of arable lands. You moved from one hemisphere to another, from a complex of several seasons to the dichotomised rainy and dry seasons of the north-westerly lands. A lighter rainy season gave way to a heavier one with one clear dry season. You thought you were exposed to a mammoth chameleon of changing colours and shapes. Groovy landscapes yielded to even more arresting ones, awe-striking you with the connectivity of the thick green forests that progressively paled into lighter green and then to dull yellow grassfields of the higher lands.

The soil, too, if you cared to throw casual glances at the exposed patches of earth, altered gradually from the wet, dark colour (humus) to bright brown. Settlements also transitioned, undulating and alternating between modern densely populated city dwellings and environments to sparsely dotted village houses of uneven thatch and quality. You noticed some magnificent village squares characterised by houses of sun-dried bricks. Their exquisitely crafted thatch roofs of raffia palms or grass, you could not miss. Unlike the city houses, the village ones varied more in designs and shapes that announced cultural significations and heritages.

But before this process of informative exposure, and while we were still in Yaoundé, we had several places to see. In the meantime, an unplanned but tartly pleasant moment interjected itself.

We were already two days in the country, and it was Sunday morning. We attended church service, as a token of gratitude, you may say, for the plenitude of blessings we already had. That is when we came upon Professor Daniel Lantum, a renowned scientist and researcher, a legendary plenipotentiary whom I knew as a student in my college years. Fate contrived for me to meet him that morning and we exchanged hearty pleasantries after a warm handshake. All of us chatted with him and took a group picture. It was, to me, more than a coincidence that I was meeting him in person after such a long time. He was a national hero, internationally recognised for his contributions to science.

***

One place to visit was the Cameroon Radio Television, the country's telecommunication broadcasting company established in 1985. Government-controlled and abbreviated as CRTV, the corporation is the government's official media channel. For one thing, it was housed in an eye-catching structure, unique in its design and massive capaciousness. The natural greenery of its surroundings belied the sophistication of the technological equipment it housed. The savvy of its personnel, the ornate designs of its furniture, and the total prestige that announced itself at every curve of the ambience made it one of the most charming places to visit.

The ground-breaking launching of the corporation took place when I was a young person, and we watched every inch of the happenings live on television. Perhaps because of the technological savvy of its crew, they made the structure look most attractive, magnificently towering over the entire city of Yaoundé. The launch and the ambience were the story in every household that had watched it for a while. Young college students looked forward to opportunities of having a guided tour of the edifice.

Although many years had passed since the launch, visiting CRTV this summer holiday was still a thrill for me as it was for our entire crew. We were all fascinated from its welcoming main doors to the multiple architectural state-of-the-art that confronted us at every curve, accentuated by its transparent glassiness. We had the leisure of more than three-quarters of an hour to explore the offices and spaces and see the dexterous personnel doing live editing at work. In the newsroom, we stayed until the last minute before leaving. We had to be out before the news was because we were not supposed to be part of the broadcast. We saw technicians deftly manipulating huge industrial broadcasting equipment from the transmission centre. We watched the schemes in the monitoring room and production studios for several programs of that day.

Memorable were the production program rooms of "Tam Tam Weekend" and "Week Night News." In my youth, I loved watching the program *Tam Tam Weekend*. It was thanks to its strong appeal that, so many years on, it was still a vibrant program for viewers. Meeting the different personnel teams was exciting. Each had its role, and you marvelled at the corporate and organic functioning of the whole. The different services merged as one network of corporate action – CRTV network corporation. We were even privileged to peep into the company's new transmission room. It was not yet completed and was yet to be launched.

At the other end of our curiosity, we also sniffed into the junk room, where obsolete equipment was piled. Our ignorance of technology did not privilege us with insights beyond the outward appearances of junk. To our unschooled common sense, the dirtier, the more obsolete, which was a somewhat naïve perspective. But I think it had its place too. The jumbled crowding of the entire stuff somewhat baffled us with its chaos as an aspect of complexity. We were lost in the sea of distinctly shaped and often polished junk.

The human component of our tour of the corporation edifice was more meaningful. Mr Robert Ekukole welcomed us to his office. We had a great time with him, dousing our curiosities. Not overtaken by officious singularity, he made us feel at home and welcome. Of course, we knew he was sacrificing much time from his daily tight schedule. But being with him in person after listening to him on radio programs and watching him on television screens for so many years was a big deal for me.

I hadn't expected to meet him, but thanks to the encounter, my appreciation of the corporation was even more heightened by the time we were through. The services for the nation with details of their untiring input were entrancing - their extensive coverage of events, whether private or public, political, religious, social, economic or physical and with in-depth thoroughness for the benefit of the state and its citizens. The day and our time soon ran out, but not before we clinched it permanently by having beautiful photos, among them those at the CRTV Name Board at the entrance gate, which we jealously guard.

* * *

**At King John Njoya's Palace, Bamunka, Ndop**

The CRTV Director encounter became a blueprint for the piquing moments we shared. After traversing the shifting climes and weather conditions, we were in Ndop. Although the town mayor's or the administrative authority's office would have been an important stopover, these were not places you went to off working hours. In any case, they didn't constitute our interest, part of our itinerary, or goal. The royal palace or, more appropriately, His Royal Highness, King John Njoya of Bamunka, Ndop in the Ngoketunjia Division of the North West Region was our port of call. He ruled the Bamunka kingdom.

It was my first view and never-before ventured visit to that kingdom. A native of Nso, another kingdom of the Grassland but much bigger, I was aware of the sacredness and decorum that had to characterise happenings in the palace. A palace was much of a sanctuary and a place of awe. The ambience of the Grassfields palaces differed only in detail; otherwise, they were the same in aura and practice. Characteristically, silent calm was expected. Then there were instruments, costumes, artefacts, music, and traditional belief systems that stood out. From the queens, princes and princesses, entrancing stories are told that explore these various characteristics of the kingdom. They repeat the expectations of how visitors and insiders of the palace are to comport themselves at the court or around the king.

The palace guards gave us a guided tour of the palace while instructing us on the rules of decorum. Even before we stepped into the palace courtyard, they made the briefings, but at each juncture, we had pre-briefings. It was a schooling in cultural mores which the items in the palace accentuated.

Inside the palace, a magnificent photo exhibition of the Kings before the reigning one struck you, particularly, King John Njoya's great-grandfather and father. The uniqueness of the piece registered itself as a specimen of remarkable worth, adding to the creativity of its setup. One couldn't help ogling at the king's throne, an ornate artefact engraved with carvings of warriors and other suggestive scenarios, which I can hardly remember. A table at the centre of the spacious room had its attractions. It was flanked by side stools that bore minutiae of elegant adornment. Even the walls were not just plane surfaces but carried sophisticated shapes and contours. These gave the entire setting a characteristic of mosaic crafting that somewhat stressed complexity rather than prettiness. However, each artefact, each item, was authentically home and culture inspired. Each subtly suggested the norms and mores, the king's authority, the kingdom's life and history, the people's *weltanschauung*, and their way and view of life.

As mentioned earlier, I had visited Nso Palace during my secondary school days when an excursion took us to that trough of items which concretely announced my cultural heritage and told the history of my people. The setup inspired awe that tilted more to fright, especially because it was also from there that the dreadful (masquerades) also emanated. We had been drilled to be terror-stricken by their appearance. Even their exploits were generally considered ruthless towards defaulters. Dread and anxiety rather than curiosity, therefore, characterised that excursion for me. So, despite the initial excitement at the novelty of the day trip and the privilege of entering the palace with its secret and sacred places, that visit hadn't been so beneficial. My innocence and naivety played their part then and I lost the fun. As I remember, we also had a tour guide who told us what to expect and do; the snag was in the preconceptions I took to the scene. They clouded the amusement.

I have already indicated that palaces of the Grassfields have many commonalities. One such commonality is that entering the sacred and usually secret places was reserved for authorised persons, often initiated persons or those who, by inheritance, had the right to do so. Because of their royal ancestry, Dr Ambrosia Kweh Mondoa and Matanda Mondoa worked it out for us to be privileged with entering what I should call the archival exhibition rooms within the palace. The absolute plenitude and wealth of what lay in those storehouses of the rich culture was overwhelming.

Being of the royal house of the Kingdom of Bamunka, Matanda Mondoa's heritage stretched generations back. Thanks to it, we were accorded direct audience with the Bamunka king at his private residence towards the end of our visit. We imbibed reserved wines and drinks and historical anecdotes and interesting tales told by the King himself. Matanda and her friends, Christina and Sarah, had their planned gift in return for the benefits they were receiving - songs to entertain the royal household that expressed appreciable delight at our visit.

Our visit was also an opportunity for the king to welcome home Princess Matanda Mondoa. Symbolic and ritual performances involving aspersions and pronouncements accompanied the welcome and blessing of the princess. This turned out to be the central piece in the entire visit to the palace of the Bamunka, converting the pleasure trip into something more emblematic.

In the yard, towering elegantly, a thing it had done for more than 100 years, swayed a tree with evergreen leaves. Its trunk was sturdy, not so gnarled, but huge and with sinuous branches. It reminded you of the complex artistry of the palace objects in general. Some awesome symmetry informed the placement of the robust branches that spread in all directions, providing significant shading from rain and shine. You instantly felt you were in the presence of an ancient, experienced, and wise mystical being. And indeed, it was the historic site of many rituals of the palace, where invocations of various spirit beings had been repeated thousands of times for so many years. It was the customary site where traditional sacrifices were made to the ancestors, where prayers and incantations were offered to God for protection, healing, and prosperity, especially the prosperity of good crop yields, safe from destructive storms. You felt a power about the place that, although it was neutral to me as a stranger, must have been protectively friendly towards the good and terrifyingly exacting justice towards those who broke the rules of the land.

\*\*\*

A safari trip it was and we were leaving no outlay unenjoyed, which is why the Ndawara Tea Estate of the Bamenda highland plateau became our next stop. Ndawara was the more recent estate. In my youth, I had visited Tole Tea Estate in Buea in the South West Region of Cameroon. As it were, Tole was the mother estate but really didn't compare with Ndawara in size and modernity. The largest of three estates that make up the Cameroon Tea Estate (CTA), including Tole and Ndu, Ndawara was host to the privately owned plantation. Unlike most estates and companies owned and run by foreign nationals, this was the property of Alhadji Danpullo, a native and esteemed richest man in Francophone Sub-Saharan Africa. His net worth stood at 547 billion FCFA, about $1 billion.

The road to the estate forked out of the one leading to Lake Oku, another attraction. It was about an hour's drive away, but it took us the whole day to savour the attractions of the vast estate field, factory, nursery, and wildlife. It was a world of its own, with winding roads and hills surrounded by villages, green forests, streams, and waterfalls. Nature was at its most luxuriant charm. Unfortunately, our tight schedule caused us to rush through the plenitude that took up some 5000 hectares of wavy hillocks and slopes. As we learnt, the breathtaking expanse was not yet at its maximum as an expansion was underway. It hosted the biggest tea nursery in the world, we were told. And even though the estate was mainly meant for tea, on it was an animal park that included ostriches, cows, horses, monkeys, and snakes, of which a ten-to-twelve-foot-long python was noteworthy.

Our savouring of the setup was enhanced by immersing ourselves in hand-picking the fresh tea, bringing it to our nostrils for the aroma before, during, and after processing. It was an experiential aspect that teased the best feelings of the trip out of us.

From the fields, we trouped to the factory and observed firsthand the entire transformation process of the tea, from fresh green leaves with succulent chlorophyll coats to the packaging of the dried, dull brown, finely ground and tea-bagged, ready-for-shipment packages of various grades of the finished product. The processing stage begins at the trough, twenty at the time of our visit. There, green leaves were prepped. Next came the rolling, where the still green leaves were crushed and moved through various processes, including oxidation, fermentation, drying, separation of the fibre, fine tea and remnants, etc., before packaging, storage, and then transportation to myriads of distribution points.

Most of the process is mechanised, using a modern-day technological masterpiece to separate the processed tea into its different grades. Watching it send out these brand grades was intriguing—the broken mixed (BM), the coarse part, and the pekoe fanning (PF) blended with pekoe dust. The inhaling of the aroma specific to the Pekoe fanning grade that was being spewed was even more captivating or rather soothing to the senses. Standing nearby, we used our fingertips to feel and sniff its strange aroma.

It was a new insight for us to learn from the training manager that it stimulated human saliva and the brain, relieving fatigue as well. Indeed, we could bear experiential witness to the facts which sounded magical. They were honest and happening to us right there. True, it did not make sense at first, and I wasn't even trying to understand why we were salivating simply from inhaling the specific aroma. The training manager specifically said, "It is a veritable stimulus at first sight," and it dawned on us and explained our experience.

The different grades of the tea were labelled (Blue, Red, and

Yellow), based on particle sizes, and the packaging too was different and included forms of sacs and sachet bags. Packaging was the last stage of the process, followed by a distribution plan, which had to be strategic and effective to ensure that the right quarters and targeted local and international destination points received what was necessary. Transportation trucks on standby readily toted. The market, besides the local, and national markets, included the entire spread of fifty-three African nations and eastern and western countries worldwide.

We noted with interest the interactive, communicative, leadership, and teamwork that characterised the employees at each juncture. A great deal of the factory work was manual, requiring many hands at each process point to handle the products or the machines.

To cap our tour, we were treated to freshly transformed brewed tea at the visitors' lounge, along with some snacks. The irresistible aroma was matched by the mildly tangy taste that made us feel so good.

As we left, we were offered gifts of tea packages of different brands and the company cloth, on which was inscribed, Cameroon Tea Estates (CTA). The tea is not yet common in the U.S. market but is well consumed in Europe and other parts of the world.

***

The beautifully serene fresh body of water known as Lake Oku generated a calming environment in a setup of natural forests that were hundreds of years old. Perhaps because of its serenity and the awe-inspiring aged environment, Lake Oku is one of the lakes associated with mystery in Cameroon. The others include Lake Awing (believed to be the lake that travels), Lake Nyos (the angry lake), and the twin Muanenguba lakes (envisaged as male and female lakes).

Mystery is not the privy of lakes only, for all bodies of water are also generally seen as conduits of spiritual forces. Forests, enclaves, hills and mountains too, in their majestic quiet command awe that teeters over the chasm of inexplicable power. The majestic awe of greatness and silent grandeur evokes the aura of the spiritual, the divine, and the mysterious.

Set in the high plateaus of the north-west highlands, Lake Oku is envisaged as sitting on top of the mountain (a double ambience of the mysterious, so to say), and in the heart of the thousands of years-old green forests of the mountain.

The panoramic view was a medley of appreciable variety that inspired connectivity with nature so original and pristine that a sense of mystery came naturally around it. But the novelty of the setup also generated instinctive curiosity and excitement amidst the perplexing wonders of mother nature that added awe to beauty. It was a captivating shift of expectations after the ranging motley of grassland, the spectacular green plains and mountain ranges, echoed by never-ending deep valleys and waterfalls. The climatic conditions at the lake environment erupted something of a surprising oasis that comprised an evergreen rainforest. But, unlike the southern forests of Yaoundé with their warm humidity, here we had a rather cold atmosphere. It felt purer in its freshness.

At 7,306 ft up Mount Oku and completely cloud forest surrounded, the crater lake must have been aeons ago. The lake lies along the country's volcanic line on a giant volcanic field measuring 62 miles in diameter, a stratovolcano, 9879 ft high. The lake surface is 600 acres, ranging from 105 to 171 ft in depth.

The only known habitat of the Oku Lake is the clawed frog; otherwise, the lake has no fish or plant life inside. Ethereally clean, its waters are considered the medicinal and ancestral home of the people who used to be called Mawes (Oku). The surrounding Kilum-Ijim Forest has been set up as a nature reserve by BirdLife International and the Cameroon Government.

First, the breathtaking massif of Mount Oku and the hilly landscape invitingly challenged you to keep climbing and then descending. The refreshing coolness of evergreen forest scenes around the lake makes it worthwhile. Solid steps and rails support body balance on your way down, the bird music from the forest splicing with the gently whistling winds to cool your moods and stir your feel-good vitality.

Three cultural communities – Oku, Kom, and Kijem – hemmed the lake. We stopped at the market square for dinner while observing the people do business. There were plenty of locally grown fresh crops, including plantains, potatoes, corn, banana, and white and brown honey (some of it still in honeycombs). A wide variety of fruits and lots of vegetables coloured the market spaces. So, we feasted our eyes no less than our stomachs, and as sunset and twilight inched in, we booked into a hotel for the night. We needed rest before the return trip over the hilly country back home. We also anticipated rain, given the perennial cold and rainy Oku environment. And indeed, it rained that night, the first rain we had had during the trip. Such a rain it was, a torrential downpour for a good part of the night. The raindrops were so heavy that it gave an impression of an avalanche of pebbles attempting to burst through the hotel's corrugated roof. Not as if I hadn't had the experience of such heavy rains before. The almost threatening novelty was more for Matanda, Christina, and Sarah. They even decided on a closer encounter by going outside and standing on the hotel's veranda for a closer look - an overwhelming combination of threat and fun.

Photo shoots added to the personal experiences of the trip to immortalise its significance. Yes, Lake Oku had been in our itinerary of tourist sites to be explored. Being one of those much talked about sights I hadn't been at, except as abstract knowledge learnt in school, I came to it with great expectations and was not disappointed. Even in the pictures of Lake Oku which I took, I can feel the bonding and beauty of the experience and can virtually relive the ambience and the events.

So profound was the lake experience. Nature's forces around and beneath the Lake Oku waters seemed to have been working on us, impressing us more profoundly than the physical spectacle it all seemed to be. Touched to the core, we simultaneously and immediately decided to make a second visit there. Not one of the crew hesitated. We went better prepared, determined to bring back mementoes to keep the experience permanent. We collected souvenirs of wildlife, vegetable and food plants, including bitter leaves. We carried away two bottles of two litres of the lake water home and eventually back home to the United States.

\*\*\*

It is about impressions I am writing, and H.E. Christian Cardinal Tumi, a household name in Cameroon, the Vatican and across the world, jumps to the fore after the Lake Oku experience, shifting my memoir to the coastal part of Cameroon. The Cardinal is in his eighties and fully alert, endowed with formidable intellectual prowess. With such a person, an encounter is sheer privilege and the topics to cover are innumerable.

Already, he is well known as both the voice and face of the people of Cameroon and beyond. He stands up for the right and denounces the wrong anytime and consistently, giving him the image of the people's priest, admired and respected by many in Cameroon. Even after retiring as Archbishop and Cardinal of the Catholic Church, the respect he has gained has been enormous. There is no attempt here to explore his reputation, which is all over in news and media outlets. Our little encounter is our interest here.

Our visit is to His Eminence Christian Cardinal Tumi at his residence in the Archdiocese of Douala, Cameroon. We paid two visits, somewhat like the two to Lake Oku, spending quite some days with him in the city of Douala in the Littoral Region. The first visit involved all five of us from the US, while during the second, we were only four of us, Christina having returned earlier to the US for academic and other imperatives. The Cardinal is a very busy man, so we adjusted each trip to fit his daily protocol during all the days we spent with him.

To focus on the second journey, we were coming in from Yaoundé, passing through several cities, including Edea and Kribi which are all recommended tourist places, particularly Kribi, a seaside city. Kribi is where Cameroon's deep-sea port is located, while Edea has the longest river in Central Africa, River Sanaga, meandering and with its spectacular waterfall. Glimpses of the scenes are visible as we ride along the road, crossing bridge after bridge. The desire for more palpable encounters with the towns is high. Unfortunately, we do not accomplish the wish to visit Kribi, our schedule of activities being tight.

The Yaoundé-to-Douala trip takes hours nonstop, with moderate to heavy traffic in some cities along the way. The weather is generally sunny, a good day for market-goers and traders. The displayed trade items of retailers, along with businesses, provide remarkable views. The movement is shaded by changes in the kind of people, their culture, food, languages, landscapes, soils, and environments in general as we glide westward and southerly from Yaoundé. Generally, we move from the milder warmth and humidity of Yaoundé to greater heat and humidity in Douala on the coast. We adapt to the changes and do as the old saying goes; in Rome, do as the Romans.

Arriving in Douala, it was a truly warm welcome we had at the Cardinal's residence. It was a new experience, even though we had visited him earlier in January 2016. It felt good to see him and be in his presence. Warm-hearted pleasantries we exchanged, and the priest had beautiful stories about his life experiences. We were rapt by his personal experiences and journeys over the years. He had lots of beautiful life and religious stories to share, including his activities as Bishop Emeritus of the Archdiocese of Douala. One thing that caught our attention was his private visit to St. Elizabeth Ann Seton Parish, Bear, Delaware in the USA in October 2012. We learnt that the visit was a collaborative effort between Africana and St. Elizabeth Ann Seton Parish to celebrate its integrated diversity as a parish and home to many Africans. Africana celebrated African heritage through food, drink, arts, dance, fashion and education with its community. The annual event is more than a dozen years on. All five crew members had been active participants and hosts during the Cardinal's visit. The success of this milestone celebration with Cardinal Tumi as a guest of honour changed the life of Seton Parish and its parishioners. Now, years later, it was time to reminisce about that visit and the impact he created on us individually and on the parish as a whole.

The food at the Cardinal's was delicious, whether at breakfast, lunch or dinner all the days we spent there. The excellent taste tempted you to want to ask for more and more. Each meal was always a full course and mealtimes were strictly observed and respected in the Cardinal's residence. Food variety ranged from huckleberry, ndole soup, cabbage with egusi, stew/tomato sauce with beef or chicken to plantain (green or semi-ripe), fufu, rice, and a lot more. Good quality wine was in a variety of colours (red, yellow, white, and other shades) during meals and for relaxation.

Mealtimes came only second to the moments spent with Cardinal Tumi who blessed everyone and the meal before and after. The time I sat at his dining table remains ingrained as a moment of honour to me. That is also when his best funny stories were recounted leaving you each time with feelings of joyful calm and gratitude for the opportunity to be in his presence in real life. A sense of humour thrust his personality, which came out fully in the stories he told, and which embodied teachable life moments, too. Always, the dining table was a leisurely time of pleasant relaxation. Dinner, particularly when work time was over for the venerable old man, was drawn out by relaxed savouring of wine and stories that roved over the horizons of geography, socio-political scenes, and various intellectual landscapes.

Punctually during the first particular, Matanda, Christina, and Sarah would provide a live orchestra for our listening pleasure. Their enchanting sounds filled the house, stirring joyous sensibilities as we listened from the comfort of cushioned seats. The young voices had all the vigour and subtle stretches of the musical scales at their command, which they further scaled up by beaming smiles, each of which seemed to be directed at us individually like a special favour. The Beatles' songs were among the favourites which they presented as a group and as individuals.

Supper over, including the wining and music, the Cardinal would pray, blessing us for the night. That is how our days ended, and we parted to our rooms at the Formation Centre. It was homely, and I felt safe and protected in that oasis of peace. It was like being at your home. The venerable man of God called us his children and we looked up to him as we would a gentle father figure. And indeed, he was our Spiritual Father as well as Family Father, his home open to everyone. To all, he gave equal opportunity to see him upon their protocol clearance.

Our first two-day sojourn at the Cardinal's was punctuated with brief trips from Douala to Buea and Kumba, both cities in the South West Region. Buea had the uniquely symbolic touristic Mount Cameroon, but we also went south to Limbe to commune directly with the Atlantic Ocean before returning to Buea and the Mountain Hotel. Most significantly, the Buea trip led us to family bonding as we called at the Mondoa family residence. This was the home of the late grannies of Matanda. It was where her father, Dr Mondoa, had grown up. The historical background added much depth of meaning to Buea Town, making it no longer a mere place visited, but a home. I had the added advantage of having lived nine years in the city and being familiar with its various quarters and tourist sights. It was nonetheless satisfying for me to share the moments there, supporting Matanda in her journey to the home of her grandparents. But it was not only the family bond that made the home worth our while. Set on the hill, with a panoramic view of almost all of Buea Town settlements, the home made the day memorable.

Since good things do not last forever, we had to leave the beautiful home with its nostalgic grip and travel to Kumba, more than one and a half hours away. Matanda's grandparents were no longer alive to keep us and to give us the homely feel in Buea.

So, there was just the sacredness of their past residence and the spirit of their ancestral protection for us to keep.

Kumba was different; another thrill of a family union as we met and spent quality moments with the retired government delegate of the city, Mr Caven Nnoko Mbelle. He was family to Matanda and the Mondoas, but co-incidentally, also a well-known figure to me, having been my high school instructor at CCAST Kumba. It was during my last year in that school that he was appointed Government Delegate of the city. Even then, he continued to be a significant figure in my life as the government delegate of the town, a public figure whom every citizen of the town knew and talked about. Having known him in those capacities and now meeting him in his residence was significant to me. He was different now, seen through the lens of a retiree in his family set-up. He was venerable, the way persons who have held high offices usually are since the dignity of office seems to follow them home to retired life and everywhere else they went. He had an aura that made you appreciate and respect him without knowing why.

With his wife, he warmly welcomed us, putting us at ease with his genially humane disposition. The hospitality he exuded culminated in a delicious lunch and excellent wine. It was a kind of celebration of our visit during which we exchanged pleasantries and conviviality. Evocative stories graced the conversational spirit that prevailed. In the later part of the evening, Matanda, Christina and Sarah treated them and us to music. Again, the music of the trio was a gift, as if nothing was to go for nothing, even at the home of this elderly couple. Mr and Mrs Nnoko Mbele were visibly delighted with the musical gift executed in the sonorous, or rather honeyed voices of the girls.

We spent the night at the Nnoko Mbelles, but at dawn, I

went to visit my family, spending two days there while the others remained at the Nnoko Mbelles. Kumba was my city too, the place where I had spent my childhood until I left for the University of Buea. Coming there after a long absence heightened the quality of the time I spent with my brothers and sister at my late mother, Mami Cleopha Tamufor's home. It felt good to be back and to breathe the air of the environment. The place evoked memories as reminiscences of small and big happenings of years past came on. Particularly, the loving memories of times lived with my mother flooded my emotions. Overall, it was a kind of re-routing experience to the profundities of passing life and its significance.

I guess the rest of the crew had a hectic time at the Nnoko Mbelles, which was the last stop in our round trip from Douala to Buea and Kumba from where we assembled once more in Yaoundé. You could say that we were gathered to say goodbye to Christina, whose vacation days had ended, whereas the rest of us still had some time at hand. We all saw her off at the Nsimalen International Airport and bade her goodbye reluctantly. After she had checked in, we kept her company till she was about to board the plane. She had a safe flight back to the US.

Now, only four of the initial five-person crew, we returned to Douala and spent more days at the Cardinal's residence. The excitement of this second visit was not mitigated by being a repeat or by duration at the Cardinal's. For one thing, Matanda's birthday came up while we were there and we made a feast of it right there. Otherwise, you could say it was the rounds of interaction, meals and tales. The birthday swelled the mementoes of pictures we took. However, we met a lot of other guests who visited the venerable old man who took pleasure in introducing us to them. This registered in my mind the value we were to him as a person, his role of shepherd aside. He valued and loved our presence, and we surveyed the vicinity, the Cathedral building, and the surrounding structures, including the formation centre. The cathedral building itself was a masterpiece of ancient architecture overlaid with a decoration that was unique to this historic monument.

The hours and days soon ran out and we left Douala once more for Buea, precisely Small Soppo where we visited some significant places.

First, we visited St. Joseph's College Sasse, which had a lot of both public and private significance. For one thing, it was among the earliest colleges of West Cameroon and became synonymous with being educated or with speaking refined English. Closer to home, it was the alma mater of Dr Mondoa, Matanda's dad. From there we made a brief but quality stop at the Buea cathedral residence of Bishop Emmanuel Bushu (now emeritus) who gave us such a swell time. Our musicians again did a few musical pieces for our pleasure, a thing the bishop appreciated greatly. Our visit over, we went to Bamenda in the North West Region, passing through Douala.

\*\*\*

### Journey Home to Bamenda, North West Region

Bamenda was the destination for reconnection with our families with all the fervid and thrilling implications. Both immediate and extended loved ones were a congestion of delights. Most of our families lived in Bamenda, Ndop, and Kumbo Towns. While the others made their way to other towns and villages, I made Bamenda my base for the rest of the vacation time. It was at my elder sister's home in Mile 2 Nkwen that I settled, from there making trips to and from Kumbo, visiting my aunties, uncle, my cousins, nieces and nephews. With these, I spent quality periods and had dinners, especially in the reputable restaurants at Kumbo Squares.

Most of the time, I had lunch of vast varieties brought by my aunts. The delicacy of the variety for me was ka'ti-ka'ti (a local preparation of roasted chicken steamed in spices and palm oil), along with huckleberry, and red (actually deep yellow) corn fufu. The meals they brought were the signal welcome or rather a celebration of my home visit and the happy moments I was spending with them. Their gesture and the entire ambience of their warmth were authentic; you knew you were soaked in their genuine and selfless love. I took those positive sentiments back to Bamenda my base.

Then I took a trip to Ndop, some forty kilometres from Bamenda, and there joined the rest of our travel crew at the residence of Mr and Mrs D.G. Kweh, Matanda's maternal grandparents. They were already there two days before my arrival, but here was home indeed, as I was visiting it for the second time in two years. For Matanda, it was her first encounter with her mother's parents, and it was significant that I was there with her.

Both parents were the incarnation of tenderest loving care; they were so protective of all of us. Despite their age, their hospitality knew no bounds. Though a generally hectic time, we had the not-so-happy occasion of visiting Granddad several times in the hospital where he was being treated for some health issues. But the sobering experience was made up for by our attending a family wedding celebration at the Bamenda Metropolitan Cathedral. We had planned and looked forward to the event which went on exceedingly well - the complex ceremonies in church, the program of activities after church, pictures, the plentiful meal, and assorted wines and other drinks were delicately conducted with success. I think of it as a rather colourful wedding, joy-packed and as a confluence of two families as well as friends and relatives to bond the couple in a communal interlacing that made the marriage truly indissoluble.

Externally, there was fanfare even in dressing. The groom's family dressed uniquely to distinguish themselves from the bride's family. Beautiful African garbs by themselves were a spectacle of designs, each different. The dressing was evocative of groups of fashion models on the runway at a celebrity event. Whether in church or at the reception, you had a panoply of fashionable beautiful clothes as if on a dress parade for your admiration. The greater thrill of the show was that we were not bystanders. We fitted among the kindred folks that spangled the setup with such exquisite spectacles of communal display.

We visited Granddad in the hospital a second time the day I returned to Bamenda and had quality time with him before bidding him farewell. I retired to my sister's home, exhausted and with sore feet while my body yearned for rest to recuperate its spent self in preparation for the return journey to the US. I had had my hair braided stylishly for the season and with my sister, shopped at the Bamenda market for jewellery as well as fashionable clothes that befitted the season and our generation. The market being a place of plenty and colour, I took delight in window shopping, a thing I had frequently done before leaving for the US. Each of the jewellery I selected was exceptional, custom made or traditionally fabricated. They were souvenirs I was going to offer to family and friends in the US upon return.

My luggage packed and ready to go, it was August 8th, 2016, and all of us reassembled in our Yaoundé domicile, prepared for departure. Our flight was scheduled for late evening. Early enough, friends and family members accompanied us to the airport. With them, we shared last fond moments while waiting to board our flight. The time came to part and emotions rose high as we bid them goodbye. It had been a twenty-four-day bonding time with these family and friends and now it was like tearing apart what had been well glued with affection. New friendships too had been made, new experiences gathered, and new emotional and physical worlds explored. But there comes a time when the best must pass away, as do the worst, and ours was the time to part ways, sweet or painful as had been.

In sum, it had been a unique experience, and no hope of replication was possible. A second or any other trip to Cameroon could surely be made, but not the peculiarities of this one just completed. Ways had to be parted and distancing wedged between the experience and us as we took off. The only lasting thing to hold to were the bits of memory enshrined in some of the jottings we all made.

**Kanla Rachel Ngeh** is career focused on Human Resources, Business Administration and Healthcare Administration. Recently, she's gained new knowledge and is passionate about Financial Literacy Education for individuals and families. She bubbles with a love for travel, studious inquiry, singing, dancing and volunteering.

CHAPTER TWO

## Matanda

## ANCESTRAL HOMECOMING

It's a trip that my family has been preparing me for decades. From the stories of "back home" to the colourful accents of my relatives, Cameroon had been a constant but distant presence in my life. All I had were words, clothes, photos from a long-begone era, and a promise from my maternal grandfather that there's a room waiting for me to stay in. 2016 was a massive year – the infamous election, *Black Panther* was announced as part of the MCU, and my first trips outside of the US in 13 years. When my mom told me about the trip we were going to take over the summer, I was excited. All those years of stories, 2 years of French classes, and an entire childhood of watching animé had prepared me for this moment. She also allowed me to take some friends with me to have some company. I already had an idea of who I wanted to bring with me – two of my long-time friends I've known since college.

First was Christina. She was a fellow student I first met at Bryn Mawr College's fencing team when I was a freshman, and she was a sophomore. The thing that stood out to me was her sense of style; she wore a distinctive blue rose in her hair, peace sign earrings, and thick winged eyeliner. I complimented her on this, and she thanked me. I ended up not joining the fencing team, instead going into belly dance, video games, interfaith clubs, and other activities. When Superstorm Sandy rolled around a year later, I was watching *Bridget Jones's Diary* in the hallway of my friend's dorm room when she came out of her room and said that was her favourite movie. We've been really good friends since then and she's kept me in the loop of the goings-on in the Main Line.[1] It was during one of my monthly trips up to the area that I decided to pop the travel question over brunch. She didn't hesitate to say yes.

Second was Sarah. After I transferred to the University of Delaware, I took classes as a continuing education student before matriculating as a first-semester junior. Much like Christina, I met Sarah through another club – Sigma Tau Delta: the English Honors Society. We had spotted each other several times through events such as National Poetry Day and Banned Books Week.[2] I frequently volunteered for the latter since comic books and manga were the most banned and challenged titles in the US at the time. But it wasn't until we shared an American playwright class with a mutual friend that we delved deeper into our friendship. During my usual pickup after work at Morris Library, Mom mentioned and invited her to the trip. I had wanted to make the invitation more formal; but I did get a chance later in the week while hosting our college radio show about what the trip will

---

1   The Main Line is a string of cities along an old train line that goes from Malvern to Center City Philadelphia. Bryn Mawr is around the Center City half of the line. If you want to get an idea of the place, watch M. Night Shyamalan's 90s films.

2   For more information, visit https://bannedbooksweek.org/.

entail and the itinerary of our stay.

As for me, there was a whole lot of personal knowledge and national pride on the line. While I am an American by citizenship and birth, my parents always emphasized my Cameroonian heritage through dress and upbringing. For a while, it did feel like I was walking in two worlds whilst trying to create a third that fit just right for me – trying to embody the things my parents taught while at the same time acknowledging my education; to be proud of the heritage I have, yet to not carry the arrogance and disregard often associated with Americans: well-meaning or otherwise. This concern of being "enough" often came out (and sometimes still does come out) as situational anxiety, but it also produced an urge to research and the desire to try to do things the right way according to the home culture. All of this certainly came to a head during the preparation, but I also had to remind myself that I was coming home to people that I hadn't seen since I was a child.

A few months prior to this trip, I went to Costa Rica for spring break. It was mainly for a volunteer mission but it had also prepared me for the climate, currency, and the possible culture shock I was going to experience in Cameroon. While it probably wasn't going to be as dramatic as the culture was in my upbringing, trying to blend in was at the forefront of my mind. The pressure was high because I wanted to make my family proud; it was important that I live up to and beyond their expectations.

I had learned French the year before. While I wouldn't call myself fluent in the language, I knew just enough to get by and communicate my basic needs. Mom also encouraged me to come up with ideas of things to do during our time there. At the top of my list was visiting relatives and family friends we hadn't seen in a long time and possibly getting some footage or recordings from them. I really wanted to see Grandpa since I hadn't seen him in person since high school and my dad's hometown. I also wanted to see my godfather who was the Prime Minister at the time. I also had a few locales I wanted to visit.[3]

Christina and Sarah went all out for this trip. Christina treated this trip almost like a band world tour; we had songs planned and prepped and we even had coordinating outfits. Sarah wanted to learn some French phrases before we went on our trip. For my contribution, I brought some anime DVDs as well as my voice-acting mic. I also helped out with the visa applications and before long, we were sitting in the middle of my living room, weighing our carry-ons and packing snacks for the long haul.

The day before the trip, our local pastor had a small Mass to pray for us to have a safe journey. After that, we had an elaborate dinner with all of our friends and family complete with all of our favourite foods. We also did some karaoke and small performances for our guests, and they had a fun time. As one final surprise, my dad gave me a new cell phone so that I could keep in touch with everybody back at home. It also was an early birthday present so that I could take a bunch of videos and photos while I was there. It ended up being a great investment as a good number of the photos in this book came from my phone. It also saved me the room and anxieties that could come with travelling with electronics.

On July 20th, we got into a rented van and rode up to JFK Airport and our flight to Cameroon. Dad followed not too far behind with a few of our bigger bags and to say his goodbyes. I

---

3   Spoiler alert – we missed quite a lot. Hopefully we get to go next time!

watched the last bunch of YouTube videos and shows I was going to access in the US until we landed in Brussels and eventually Yaoundé. It was a great distraction from the nerves of being in another place outside the Americas and Europe for the first time. I know how to handle a long flight but I know the biggest struggle was going to be sleeping on the plane. But even before that, there is the one thing that every nerd dreads – the check-in.

I keep my passport and boarding pass close to my person as I go through the line. I bring the giant bags to check in followed by my carry-ons. I tried not to show my nervousness. We had weighed our bags relentlessly the night before to make sure that our check-in didn't have a hitch. But the one thing we didn't factor in was the weight units were in kilograms, not pounds. As a result, while our checked bags were fine, my carry-ons were overweight. I always keep my electronics in my carry-on because I've heard of too many travelling horror stories growing up where people put their electronics in checked bags and were left with a bag clearly broken into or their items disappeared. The service person I had almost took pleasure in the dilemma I was facing on which things to sacrifice to the check-in gods. It took all of my strength to not go into a complete meltdown in the middle of the terminal. I ended up having to transfer my voice-acting mic and my laptop to one of my checked bags as they were the heaviest items on my person. Later on in our trip, we figured out the reason why it registered as heavy despite having minimal items was the bag itself. It's robust and ideal for domestic trips – not so much international. Thankfully, the security check went much more smoothly, so I could forget the rough experience. Christina reminded me that this was JFK – of course, they were going to be much stricter than other airports like Newark or Philly.

Even though my laptop and mic were spirited away with my baggage, I still had my iPad, my phone, and some books to keep me distracted. There was also the movie list which I was going to take full advantage of as I have a lot of trouble sleeping on planes due to the lack of back support (unless you're first class of course). I re-watched T*he Martian*, *The Revenant*, and checked out a French film called *Lolo* starring Julie Delpy. Between the lack of lumbar support and the surreal excitement that the trip was actually happening, it was hard for me to sleep. To be honest, I have trouble sleeping almost anywhere but a bed, unless I'm really exhausted. However, I can sleep on any floor pretty well! Eventually, exhaustion did carry me, and I slept for at least a couple of hours before the warm beverages and the sun shining over Belgium greeted me.

We came to the terminal a bit exhausted but also ready for the next part of our trip. Cameroon was very close, and the travel was not going to be as long as the flight from the US to Brussels. Being in Belgium, of course, we had to try traditional Belgian waffles. For me, it wasn't my first time having them. I had liege waffles made by a Main Street café called the Perfect Blend. Sadly, they shut down permanently in April 2020 due to the financial strain of the COVID-19 pandemic. We had a couple of hours to stretch and layover before we got to the next flight, so we enjoyed our simple breakfast and then went to the transfer terminal by bus. I saw plans to do something similar to the local airports in the US – given the very international nature the world has become lately; it would make sense to do transportation like this to make getting to your proper terminal a lot easier to achieve. Treadmill paths can only take you so far in expediting your trip to your plane.

We jump onto the second plane to take another seven-hour

flight to Yaoundé with a brief stop in Douala. The excitement was palpable as we got closer, and the first sight of the rivers emerged from the windows. The trees were very tall, and they had a slight fog from the clouds. Up until the second half of the trip, I was in such a state of disbelief that I felt like I was in a picture book. I still have the photo of that first sight in my album. But I was ready to go to the place where I was always told stories of growing up.

We landed in the Yaoundé Airport and picked up our bags. We met my cousin Louis at the airport, and he, along with a friend, had a truck waiting for us to take us to our apartment. Mom and Auntie Rachel got into one truck while Sarah, Christina, and I got into another. The exhaustion of the two flights and the time zone difference was starting to catch up to me, so I nodded off for a few minutes. I managed to wake up just enough to see the first sights of the city. It was bustling much like New York City. Outdoor markets, barbecues, street vendors, and clubs were all lit up for the night. An abundance of bikes and cars travelled through the streets. There was a very light amount of traffic lights and control, but every driver and pedestrian seemed to intuitively know what to do.

But at one choked juncture, the truck had to be readjusted. I recalled a couple of people warning us in the middle of the street. And then…BOOM! The truck backed into a deep drain that would be considered a ditch or pothole back in the US. It was going to take a team to lift it out. Thankfully, we were not too far from the apartment, so after Mom and Auntie Rachel were dropped off, we were picked up and brought to our final destination.

We passed by the presidential residence followed by the main square. Then we took the right path of the road where we passed a series of restaurants and palm trees. After a huge stretch of wall, a right turn is made, leading us through a precariously narrow path atop a steep hill – after all, we are in a mountainous region much higher than the land I had called home for the longest time. Once the gate opened, we knew that we had arrived.

My mother had rented out an apartment for almost a month. It was a five-room space complete with a living room, dining room, a fully functional kitchen, and WiFi access. Auntie Balki, a Mandela fellow we had met just earlier in the year, as well as Louis's fiancée, Melanie were waiting for us at the house with food and a warm welcome. We had a couple of invitations for the next day – first was a graduation ceremony at a local school. The second was visiting the prime minister – my baptismal godfather. Both things would happen in the early morning hours so we would be able to rest by the afternoon.

After dinner, we packed our things in our respective rooms and the snacks we brought into cabinets. My mom and Auntie Rachel shared one room, Christina got a room to herself, and Sarah and I shared a room. We all had our separate mattresses. Our welcoming party leaves for the night, we settle in. I switch into my pajamas and close my eyes. And just when I felt like I could relax into the mattress with open arms…

BZZZZT!

My eyes whiz open. This was a buzz that sounded all too familiar, but I was hoping to avoid it during this vacation. I tried to curl up into another position and slip into dreamland once more. But once again coming through my ears…

BZZZZT!

Mosquitoes. The reminders of all of the WHO and NHS advisories about yellow fever and Zika came back to the forefront. We were required to get yellow fever vaccines as well as having to take antimalarials every day for the duration of the trip. Zika was more a Central and South American pandemic than an African one, so the concern was overdone in retrospect since I wasn't in any of the at-risk categories. I pulled out the bug spray I placed underneath the bed and sprayed myself and my surroundings. The buzzing continued. The mosquitoes also started to annoy Sarah, so we tried switching rooms and spraying more bug spray. No luck. Eventually, we had to cover our heads and try to get to sleep – that didn't happen until 1 am when exhaustion eventually took over; we were expected to go out to the embassy at 6 am. We didn't know until the 3rd day that the window was open and that's why our near sleepless night occurred.

Sarah and I were pretty groggy the next morning while Mom, Auntie Rachel, and Christina looked much more chipper. Mom reassured me that we'd have time to sleep in after all of the meetings were over. I tried to shake off the exhaustion as I put on my dress and sweater for the day. Louis and Melanie picked us up from the apartment to go to a nursing school graduation ceremony. We showed up pretty early, but a lot of activity was happening outside of the centre. Many officials and attendees lined the parking lot, and a band of drummers and horn players announced the grand nature of this occasion. We took the time to take some selfies as this was our first day in the country. But not too long after we got settled into the ceremony, we had to leave for our appointment with the Prime Minister of Cameroon. Thankfully it was close by.

It was the first time I had seen my godfather since he was elected. He has been a close family friend and has supported my parents during their times of need. He was also instrumental, along with my late godmother, in ensuring my survival when

I was born prematurely. He was the Cameroonian ambassador to Canada for a long time, but he never let the position control his relationships. When I was a child visiting Canada for the first time, he took me around his favourite places in Ottawa and Montreal, much like a father or an uncle would for his children. Even behind a number of officers, desks, secret elevators and waiting rooms he had as Prime Minister; I knew he still had that kind heart. But I also knew that several years had passed since his ambassador days, and whether we want to admit it or not, power can change a person, be it voluntarily gained or involuntarily thrust. All of this was going through my mind as I was waiting in the reception room. While the photo my friends and I took together seems to show relaxation, deep down I was going through a small mental spiral of wanting to prove I was properly grown up and the hope that deep within the title and position of Prime Minister that my godfather was on the other side. Thankfully I didn't have to think about this for too long as the secretary invited us into his office.

The room was lined with brown leather sedans leading up to the head of the room with its own sedan framed with two elephant tusks and the bright yellow, red, and green of the Cameroonian flag on its pole. A portrait of the President - possibly from the 70s or 80s based on the blue background - sat right above the sedan. Standing in the middle of the room was my godfather. As soon as the secretary closed the door, it felt like we were continuing where we left off in our relationship – still warm and tender and with the sense of humour I know and love. He had aged significantly since the last time we had met. But he also had the sharp wit and conversational points of a veteran ambassador.

This is where I'm sorry to say it gets to the disappointing

bit where I'm like Bilbo Baggins at the end of *The Hobbit*.[4] The jet lag combined with the disturbed sleep from the night before and the cosiness of the sedan finally caught up to me at last and I nodded off in the middle of the meeting. I managed to say small things about what I was doing in school and what I was looking forward to experiencing in Cameroon, but I couldn't keep up with the conversation for long. I know Christina was especially engaged and I was grateful for her presence because clearly, I wasn't one hundred percent present. But after the small nod, I had enough energy to get back in. It got to an interesting conversation about ancient Mediterranean history. This was also the big stroke of luck and privilege that comes with being related to a person of power, and my friends and family understood my situation because if I were any more average than I already was, I probably would've been criticized for the rest of my life!

After all of the pleasantries and catching up were done, my godfather gave us presents of his favourite green tea[5] and bars of Cameroonian dark chocolate. We had spent almost two hours in his office, and he looked forward to seeing us again in the middle of our trip. We sang *Seasons of Love* from the musical *Rent* and said our goodbyes before proceeding back down the secret elevator to the real world. We then took some photos in front of the office and the fountains before Louis came to drop us back in the apartment. I stripped off the semi-formal wear

---

4    For those who haven't read Tolkien's work, his first book in the Middle Earth universe was a children's novel called *The Hobbit*. Without spoilers, it's obvious that the story leads up to a massive battle at the end. The main character Bilbo Baggins gets knocked out right at its beginning. Because the story is told through his perspective, he wakes up at the battle's aftermath and everything is tied up in a short summary. It's nothing like the final movie *Battle of the Five Armies*!

5    I still have it in my pantry!

as fast as I could before I jumped into bed and napped off the remaining sleep deprivation. Melanie and Auntie Balki delivered more home-cooked food for lunch and dinner, as well as some groceries for breakfast.

While I was napping, Mom did our currency exchange from American dollars to Cameroonian Francs. It was a really funny experience because all of us had never held so many bills in our hands before. But thanks to my experience in Costa Rica, I knew that the sensation of holding a lot of bills gives us the illusion that we have a lot of money when it really wasn't worth much – everything was going to go quickly. So, I treated my money much like how I treated my Costa Rican colonés – with respect to the place and a tight budget. It also helped that CFA and colonés are a 1:1 conversion so it was pretty easy to figure out how much we had. But at that moment, I felt like having fun with my friends. A couple of my favourite photos from the early part of this trip happened here - Christina's wide smile as she's holding the francs in her hands while Sarah is holding a meme-worthy surprise face mixed with wonder. The follow-up photo in my album has smiles all around with me holding my own set of fanned-out francs like a Roaring 20s Beyoncé knockoff.

I played a little bit of the mobile port of *Phoenix Wright: Ace Attorney* and started taking advantage of the abundance of Netflix titles abroad before nodding off for the night.[6] This time, the mosquito buzzing was nowhere to be found, thanks to the new wall repellents installed and the now-shut window.

The next day was a rest day, so we decided to check out the

---

6  This is what happens when America puts every piece of intellectual media behind company paywalls – another excuse to travel abroad. Thank goodness VPNs get mass produced a few years later.

National Museum in Cameroon.[7] After having a simple breakfast of hot chocolate, tea, bread, fruit, and eggs, Mom called us a taxi to ride there. The locale was set up for a summer concert series and was just about to start up a film festival in the next week. The museum used to be the presidential residence up until the 1970s. Its structure was reminiscent of classic German architecture down to the marble floors, courtyard, and levels. The structure and material make you feel that this building was built to last forever, even in the tropical mountainous climate.

We weren't allowed to take pictures in the museum. We did get a guided tour of the various exhibits. It was an exploration of the various aspects of Cameroonian culture and history – from colonialism and independence to its present and the art, languages, and ethnic groups that came along for the ride. It was more fascinating to witness the rapport between the tour guide and my mother. I had no idea that she had such a depth of knowledge and involvement in a lot of these life-shaping moments. There were small things she would correct or supplement because of first-hand experiences and anecdotes. This was stuff that I definitely would not have learned in a classroom, no matter how well-read the teacher is. We spent almost the entire day in the museum, from opening to closing time, and we explored a good amount of the building. By the time we came out of the museum, the sun had begun to set so we took advantage of the light and took as many photos as possible in the courtyard with the absence of interior photos. There were a series of bronze statues representing the various ethnic groups in Cameroon. Two spiders guarded the stairwell into the museum.

---

[7] I discovered later that it had just opened the year we arrived. We came at a good time!

A queen next to a panther sits in front of the building, showing the colonial structure who is the true boss of this kingdom. Two years later, a photo of one of the spider guardians was published in Caesura - my university's English department magazine. I also found out on my second trip to Cameroon in 2019 that the panther is a symbol of royalty. To bring one alive or present its pelt was a sign of honour. Can everybody say "Wakanda forever"?

The museum gave me the right space to ask the questions that I wasn't able to ask with the right words and context in America. Now that I have been to the country twice, I feel more comfortable asking more instead of the distant imagination of Cameroon that I had years earlier.

The next day we were invited to Louis and Melanie's church for mass. The same day, one of my mom's friends surprised us with a driver for the rest of the trip. His name is Mr. Gilbert, and he was a professional driver. He soon became a part of our family as we shared meals, and he suggested even more locations we never considered or heard of. I'm so happy that we gained another friend on this journey, and we still keep in touch with each other to this day.

Since we were staying in the French speaking side of the country, the entire mass was in French. This was where I hit my fluency limit as religious terms are not really a part of the college curriculum unless you're learning curse words in Québecois, which are Catholic sacraments due to the Protestant history of the country. But the one bright side of growing up Catholic is that regardless of language fluency, you can still have an idea of what is going on in the Mass. There were also some aspects that were familiar due to special Masses done in the US by the African community. The Bible procession and the walk-up offertory were the two stand-out moments. After the mass was over, we came across one of Mom's old friends who she had not seen in a few decades.

Mom had a friend who worked at the CRTV broadcast station, so she made an appointment with him to allow us to tour the facilities. The building was built in the 1960s by the Siemens Corporation - yes, the same one that also builds Bluetooth, sound, and medical devices. It now serves as the national broadcast station and it was where we met Mr. Robert Ekukole, my mom and dad's friend. We explored the editing room, the research station, and even the set of a morning show. He wanted to broadcast us on the air later on that day but due to time constraints and some personal concerns, we ultimately couldn't take up his offer.

We were going to my maternal grandparents' home in Bamenda through Bafoussam in a couple of days. Mr. Gilbert decided to treat us to a night-time tour of Yaoundé. We drove around the town, seeing the life that the daylight often hides - small corner clubs with rainbow lights, outdoor terraces with string lights where young and old people are drinking together, bright LED marquees promoting their various wares, and people grilling food outdoors. We picked up some grilled chicken and fish for dinner. It made a simple yet delicious and satisfying meal combined with the abundance of fried plantain and Cameroonian sodas back in the apartment.

A day before we started on our way to the village, Mr. Gilbert took us to lunch in town. It was a dish we had during our first day – roasted chicken with onions, green peppers, mayo, and fried potatoes. It sounds like a simple dish, but it would be difficult to replicate even with my culinary skills. It was clear from the unique flavour that this was a local dish that this establishment had done for a long time. The interior reminded me of some offbeat corner restaurants I would go to at home – high benches and tables, mostly white interior, mirrors to make the room seem larger than it actually was, and new TVs and rainbow LEDs lining the walls.

While we were eating, my friends and I observed the programs being played on the TV. One was programmed to the CRTV network while the other two were on two different music videos – one from the US [the Weeknd's *Earned It*] and the other from Cameroon [unfortunately, I can't remember the artist]. It provided a fascinating discussion about media standards across borders. Christina noted that Cameroonian music videos tend to focus more on narrative or prowess whereas American music videos, while they may have narratives, tend to focus more on beauty standards and attraction. It then led to a discussion of beauty standards and the value of skills in the entertainment industry. Even though I was on summer vacation, my nerdy brain never really turned off. My friends and I spent a lot of the trip talking about movie and TV theories – mostly in the direction of *Star Wars* since *Episode VIII* was released later that year. Sarah even wrote up some crossover fanfic, looked up a bunch of memes on Tumblr, and found parody songs and YouTube videos during the duration of the trip.

The chicken and potato dish is a delicacy unique to Cameroon. It has a taste that to this day I still remember – the sharp and astringent taste of the onions along with the heat of the peppers was accented by the smokiness and spiciness of the fresh grilled chicken. The fries had the right satisfying crunch on the outside, softness on the inside, and topped with unique spices and homemade mayonnaise. It's a dish I want to have the next time I come to Cameroon.

We left the apartment early the next morning. We didn't

have much time to grab breakfast as we had to make a swift departure to avoid heavy traffic. I have experience with long trips so I know how to keep myself occupied for long stretches of time. I listened to a lot of music, read almost all of the books I brought with me from home, and watched movies, TV shows, and YouTube videos I downloaded beforehand at the apartment. I even brought blankets and neck pillows to keep myself comfortable for the entire trip.

But my struggle was not in comfort; it was falling asleep. I can sleep almost anywhere as long as there is a way to get as close to horizontal as possible. I struggle with sleeping upright in vehicles unless I'm extremely exhausted – and even with that, I don't get much rest. That makes bus and car travel especially difficult. The SUV was spacious enough for us to put our stuff in and sit. But when all of the seats were occupied, I had to be creative to find a comfortable sleeping position. Even with all of the comfy pillows and blankets I had at my disposal, I ended up craning my neck past the headrest most of the time. While it wasn't the best for my neck, it at least gave my head and body the illusion that I was lying down and so I could sleep.

The Cameroonian interstate is different from an American one. Unlike in the US where there are multiple segments to get from one place to the other, it's one long stretch until you get to major cities or towns. The drive was going to be an eight-hour ride. The road was bumpy at some sections and Mr. Gilbert had to curve around various hills and potholes. Seeing the terrain outside made me realize how much more diverse the terrain was compared to my home state. In Delaware, there were not that many hills; most of the terrain landed right at sea level. Pennsylvania had more variety between the Appalachian Mountains and Lake Erie. Being above the equator also provided us with intense summers, cold winters, rainy springs, and blustery autumns. In contrast, Cameroon sat right in the middle of it all – moderate temperatures all around and two seasons my mother would tell me in bedtime stories – the rainy and the dry. Most of the areas we travelled to were about 5,000km above sea level. The richness of the country's soil was due to its ancient volcanoes. Beyond the linguistic "split" of Anglophones and Francophones, there was a diversity of people, flora, and fauna all around us.

Two hours into our trip, we took a pause to stretch our legs. My mother mentioned a spot that my grandfather took her and her siblings to when she was a kid. Mr. Gilbert knew the place since his family lived in the region. The spot seems in the middle of nowhere at first; almost the equivalent of Cowtown in New Jersey.[8] There were various farms as far as the eye could see. Across the road, there was a banana farm. But if you look at the ground, you realize one path is different from the farm itself. As you walk forward, there is an old concrete pavilion. Next to it is a set of steep stone steps. You go down and at the end is a river and a waterfall. My mother told stories about the waterfall, some of them sounded like something out of a horror video game or an artistic history book talking about the echoes of colonialism and indigenous history.

We arrived in Bafoussam around the late afternoon and headed to the market. We barely had breakfast and so we needed some respite from the hunger. But we also had the need to use the bathroom. We came up to an old stall that had seen better days. The floor was corroded from multiple travellers passing by, and the doors dangled from their hinges – it looked like one light

---

[8] Cowtown is an area in New Jersey famous for its ranches, cowboy shops, and rodeos. Getting there means crossing through long stretches of farmland.

touch would make it slam on the ground and shatter whatever remained. The old stall manager noticed that my friends and I were not from here, so she tried to clean up the stalls as best she could. But at that point, our need was greater than the building's state, so we did our business quickly.

I pulled out some wipes and sanitiser to keep ourselves clean. Mom contributed some francs to the lady to help towards proper maintenance. Whenever my mom and I recall this experience, we often look at this with a strange sense of humour. To this day I couldn't figure out the source of our laughter – was it from the absurd nature of a practical circumstance, our neutral reactions of where we would overreact or complain in any other case, or just how set we were in doing what we needed to do?

While Mr. Gilbert and my mom were getting snacks, Christina and I noticed a couple of cats crossing the market. Her cat Greta and her dog Daisy passed about a month before the trip, so she was still going through some deep grief. But seeing those cats gave her some hope that they were in touch with her.

After that magical sight, we went through the last leg of our journey, which was the bumpiest ride I had ever experienced outside of an amusement park. The SUV had a 4-wheel drive, but that wasn't enough to reduce the bouncing and bumps we endured for the last hour. It shook the vehicle so hard that I think I smacked against the window a couple of times even with gripping the handle and using my neck pillow as a shock absorber. By the time the bumps ended, we all looked like we could've used aspirin to relieve the impending headaches. We arrived at my grandfather's compound in Bamenda just before sunset, where my grandmother, my cousins, and my aunts all came to greet us. We also met with my cousins, Darrel and Leo and my grandfather's sister. Christina wanted to lie down and rest, so my grandmother guided her to her room. Sarah and I had some food and refreshments before we brought our bags into the house.

When my grandfather had his last visit to the US in my high school freshman year, he told me that when I visited the compound, he would have a room specifically for me to stay in. He also would take me around the town and show me his favourite places. The promise finally came true eight years later. Sarah and I had separate beds in one room while my mother and Auntie Rachel had another. It would be the first time I would sleep under a mosquito net. Outside of watching documentaries, I haven't used one before. We were going to my granduncle's estate in Bamenda the next day.

My grandmother brought out some buckets of warm water for us to take our showers in. It was a throwback to my childhood when my mother and I would use a bucket or unused Tupperware containers to pour water over myself to rinse off the soap. This was not strange to me at all, so it was rather easy to do. While I was taking my bucket shower, I was surprised by a tiny yellow frog on the shower wall. I was surprised at first by the sight of the little creature, but I knew better than to scream as while we were in a building, it was ultimately its home. I wanted to take a picture of it, so I took my shower as quickly as possible. But by the time I came back to the bathroom with my cell phone, it was gone. But I had a feeling it was not going to be the last time I was going to see it.

My granduncle is a king, and we were visiting one of his palaces in the area before going to his reception room. It was a huge compound complete with an in-house farm and several rooms – each one older and more ornate than the last. My mother and some of the palace attendants described some of the stories about the leaders and how they were crowned into the role. Some were kidnapped and forced into taking the throne. Nowadays, the leaders are elected, as was the case with my granduncle and my great-grandmother. I've been selected as next in line for the throne. The position I currently have is akin to a queen or, more accurately, a female king. It's more of a cultural or ceremonial position, but it was still very important for the preservation of the culture and the land. An accurate equivalent of what the title does is like that of an indigenous elder rather than the Queen of England or Ubud. There's a lot that I'm still learning about this aspect of my family and ancestry. But I hope to fill this void with future trips and discussions.

We came across one of my dad's former patients, Uncle Patrick. Mom was really happy to see him as the circumstances of his recovery sounded very harrowing. He was doing very well health-wise, and he was working in the palace part-time. Mom spent some time catching up with Uncle Patrick and I was distracted taking more photos and playing some mobile games. But before we got to the reception area, the palace's power went out. Costa Rica has helped me adapt to unexpected power outages in the tropics, so this felt like nothing new. When the staff realized it was going to be a while before they could restart the generator, my granduncle decided to have us come in even with the lack of power.

My granduncle prepared a huge spread of snacks, cookies, and drinks for us. I was ready to help serve some to my friends and my mom before getting some for myself. But the palace staff immediately stepped in and served all of us. Outside of restaurants and family gatherings, I wasn't used to having that kind of attention in what was going to be a casual discussion - at least as casual as it could be in a palace.

My granduncle discussed how he was crowned and some of the things I may inherit through his position. He also promised me that he'd show me some of the parcels set aside for me since I'm next in line. My friends looked at me with surprised faces. They often remark about how big of a deal it is and how I often act like it's not a big deal. I understand the gravity of the situation, but it's a surprise for me too; it's a degree of power I'm not used to having and, even with the best education, probably never will. In the United States, Cameroon, and even among loved ones, I often feel like I'm in-between somewhere: very American for the Africans, very African for the Americans. Super nerdy and intellectual for the average person, probably not enough for some academic circles despite my credentials. Living such a down to earth life but I have a culturally significant position coming - be it by choice, inheritance, or a mixture. All of this is a dance and it's something that certainly came to a head several times on this journey.

The next day, we drove up to Mount Oku. A bunch of horned cows were walking up the road. I was trying to find the farmer until I figured out the cows were self-directed; the farmer was much further up the road. They were very independent and organized in their own herd. We arrived at the first summit of the mountain at the Ndawara Tea Estate. We stretched our legs at the field before we toured around the factory and the menagerie full of primates, emus, and snakes. After the tour was complete, we were taken to an office above one of the production lines. The tannins and perfume from the roasting tea were very strong. Then a couple of employees came in with bolts of fabric and enough boxes of tea to survive the apocalypse – a fantasy that became very true in 2020 when the lockdown occurred, and the stockpile got heavily used. I still have a few boxes left. I also learned from Mom that the owner of the estate was one of Auntie Balki's uncles.

After our visit, we went up to the top of Mount Oku and walked all the way down to the mountain lake, which was fascinatingly calm and massive before the mountain fog started climbing over the ridge. A mountain hamlet and science centre were in the process of being built at the top. The roads were much smoother since the Prime Minister is from this region. We stayed in Oku much longer than expected so we ended up staying at a mountain hotel for the night.

Thanks to Mr. Gilbert, we had fresh roasted chicken, vegetables, and stew for dinner. I was so full that I knew I was going to rest well. But we clearly didn't think this trip through as we didn't pack many long-sleeved shirts or any outfits suitable for cold weather - the biggest sign that we came from a different climate. Mom had talked about it while we were packing, but we thought it was going to be much warmer since we were in the tropics in the middle of the summer. Thankfully the hotel owner brought us blankets and warm water in buckets to keep us comfortable overnight. Then there was heavy rain that looked like gigantic sheets of water were coming down – nothing like what we experienced in the US. We used our flashlights to see how large the raindrops were. My friends and I stayed on one side of the hotel and my mom, Mr. Gilbert, and Auntie Rachel stayed on the other. They were having a lot of fun watching us experience this weather for the first time.

The next morning reminded us of the mountain conditions. I woke up and it was as cold as a late winter day. I did bring a couple of jackets, but they were inadequate for the low temps. The blankets the hotel owner brought up were a great help. We had some empty water bottles with us, and we decided to bring a small souvenir of Oku with us. Mr. Gilbert, Sarah, Auntie Rachel and I went back up to the mountain and collected some water from the lake. We had a feeling that the water was special in some way. If it was not due to the nature of the volcano or the stories surrounding the lake, it certainly was significant to us. Nowadays I drink it when there are significant occasions or accomplishments such as birthdays, graduations, and class completions. My mother bought some raw mountain honey at the base of the mountain then we made our way back to Bamunka. The heavy rain from the mountains continued onto the compound and Sarah, Christina, and I were having a lot of fun collecting the rainwater in the buckets we had on hand.

Those days in Oku and the following day back in the compound produced some of my favourite photos from the trip. We all felt so relaxed and carefree, like children, and we were just having fun where we were at that moment. I hadn't laughed like that with friends in a while. Looking at the photo where we were trying to collect rainwater over a bucket reminds me that I am capable of feeling that way again even with challenging moments like the election and the pandemic. It was our last day in Bamunka before we went to Douala to visit Cardinal Tumi, so we relaxed as much as possible in Grandpa's compound. We also explored my uncle's farm, where he had his own chickens, turkeys, honey-making bees, and various devices to collect fresh rainwater. I didn't realise how appealing country life had been for me until then. I was still aware of how much work and dedication it would take to maintain such a life - my family has a square foot farm in our backyard, and I watched *Only Yesterday*. But I still love it, and this is an aspect of my trip that I still keep to this day.

We rested a couple more days in my grandpa's compound

before we went back to Yaoundé. On our departure day, we sang some songs for my grandparents then we started on the long ride back to the city. It was much easier to tolerate now that we knew what to expect on the trip and the bumpy ride was at the beginning of the ride rather than the end. We stopped to visit Mr. Willie Kimbeng, one of Grandpa's oldest friends. He gave us some time to stretch our legs and regaled us with stories and refreshments. He had visited us several times in the US and kept in touch throughout our stay. He also gave us some advice on how to navigate the wi-fi. After we had our fill, we continued back to Yaoundé and arrived around sunset. But we were not done with our travels – we were going to travel to Douala the next day and it was going to be much earlier and more rigorous than the last trip. We had to prepare just as soon as we arrived as we had to wake up at 4 a.m.

As I'm not a morning person, you can imagine how travelling in the early hours would be. We brought our light bags and some snacks for the road. We needed to avoid the congested traffic on the newly constructed bridge; we did still get caught in the traffic, but we managed to pass through it quickly because of our early start. Exhaustion caught up to me and I napped for most of the ride. One of my mother's childhood friends was on the way so we stopped by there to say hello and have some refreshments. My memory for words is not the best, but what I do remember the most is the fun, her favourite yoghurt drink, and her kindness. She gave us her daughter's phone number and address in the US to keep in touch with her when we get back. Sarah forgot her notebook and her cell phone in the living room. We came back to pick up the former before leaving for Douala, but we had a hard time tracking down the latter, and we couldn't come back for it as we had too intense of a schedule to make a second return trip. However, Auntie mailed it to a mailbox near our destination and we were able to pick it up a few days later. Sadly, this was the first and last time I was going to see her as she passed away a year after our trip. However, her hospitality and her gentleness will be things I'll never forget.

We arrived in Douala and the Cardinal's residence. He was clearly excited to see us as when we just stepped onto the porch, he was the one to open the door and greet us. I hadn't seen him in person since he came to the US in 2012. Since it was Sarah and Christina's first meeting with the Cardinal, there were a lot of questions and discussions. Some of the theological conversations - one of which was about the nature of sin and what counted as sin in Catholicism - became the basis of one of Christina's fiction stories, which allowed her to go for a writing program in Sicily.

Cardinal Tumi had us stay for dinner and sleep in the compound for the night. Chef David made some of the best pasta and potatoes I had ever tasted. Mom stayed in a room near the Cardinal's home while Christina, Sarah, and I stayed in a dorm building near the cathedral and the neighbouring boarding school. The room felt like a convent cell - it had a bed with a mosquito net, a desk, and a bucket for washing near the small balcony. Outside the window, I could see a small forest area along with a few more school buildings as well as some apartments. I was pretty nervous about accidentally locking my stuff in the dorm on the way to breakfast. But it wouldn't have mattered if I didn't get enough sleep. So once again, I wrapped my bed with the mosquito net and slept as much as I could.

After breakfast and an early morning private Mass, we drove to Buea to the Mountain Hotel. Much like its namesake, it was at the base of the summit of Mount Cameroon. The shift of climate and altitude could be felt as we drove up between popping our ears and the increasing chill and freshness of the air. The place itself is structured much like a high-end ski hamlet and lodge in Canada. An extensive renovation was taking place in the compound, but the major areas were repaired. It was obvious it was going to be a comfortable stay. This is where the heaviest German and British influence occurred and not too far from the hotel was an estate where the British royal family used to stay when visiting the country – it was almost 200 years old and still intact with the extreme conditions.

Mom had to go in by herself to reserve the rooms because she had a feeling if my friends and I walked in with her, they'd make the room rates steeper because we were Americans. At first I was appalled – why would our nationality raise the rates? Then I swallowed up that inquiry because I figured it out rather quickly. Americans who travel this far out would be considered to have a higher price bracket and so it's natural to charge higher. Because most would be unfamiliar with the currency exchange, travellers wouldn't know the difference if they were overcharged. We also wouldn't have the protections of this country even if we did notice either. To call out that would be the presentation of the very arrogance we were infamous for. So, I kept my mouth shut and stayed inside the car until she returned. It turned out the hotel was managed by one of my father's childhood friends and so we had a good discount. However, this luck of the dodge was going to run out and it happened here.

Christina needed to rest since the altitude shift affected her ears. Sarah and I went ahead and explored some of my father's old haunts. We drove past the teaching college my mother attended and first met my paternal grandmother. We also passed where my father first worked as a doctor before coming to the US. Eventually, we got to the final destination – St. Joseph's College:

my father's preparatory school. We weren't able to go inside the buildings since they were closed for the break, but we were able to walk around the outside. I had heard stories about the school, and I had some ideas of how the place would look, but it made it more solid with visiting the place. The campus was almost 80 years old. The buildings were in good condition, but some parts had clearly seen better days. The dampness of the mountain air and the Atlantic Ocean had made some paths difficult to traverse even with the grips of our shoes. On the cathedral side of the campus, there was a steep view of the Atlantic down below. The fog was rapidly coming in, so Mom had us go back into the SUV to continue to our next destination.

There was a priest on the outskirts of Buea who Mom wanted us to visit. He was recently installed and had a small office in the middle of a farming compound. Between the rich greenery and the lack of traffic and housing surrounding the area, it almost seemed like the middle of nowhere. It also was the middle of the afternoon, but it looked like we were the first visitors of the day. We discussed a little bit about his post. Sarah decided to perform the song *Popular* from the Broadway musical *Wicked*, and he really enjoyed it. He wasn't the only one as it turned out during our visit that a small crowd was sitting in the waiting room and heard her performance. They applauded as soon as they saw us walking out, then we rode back to the hotel. Sarah, Mom, and I took a nap for a few hours to recover. I also gave the jacuzzi in our room a shot since I'd never tried one before. I'm a good swimmer but I'm a total novice in the home aquatics department. It was a fun and relaxing experience even with the brief clumsiness with the jets.

We later dressed up for dinner in the grand dining room. Mom wanted us to perform in the hotel to practice for a casual open mic in Kumba, a small coastal town near one of the top 10 rainiest places on Earth. While we were waiting for dinner, we sang a few songs from the musicals we knew by heart. Our dinner fare was simple - some steamed local vegetables and shrimp cooked in garlic butter. Considering shrimp is part of the country's namesake - an Anglicized spelling of a Portuguese phrase meaning "shrimp river", I shouldn't have been surprised that I would have one of the best seafood dishes in existence.

The next day, however, was when some of the most challenging aspects of the trip occurred. The pressure to be "good enough" to be there really reared its ugly head. I had an intense anxiety attack in the hotel due to the stress of the incoming gig. It turned out not to be a non-issue as the venue fell through in providing a time for us to perform. So, we went straight to the home of another one of Mom's long-time friends: a person who I liked to call Uncle Gordon. His name is actually Uncle Caven; my guess is I started calling him Uncle Gordon because his moustache looked similar to the actor who played Gordon in Sesame Street. I hadn't seen him since I was very small. We had dinner and tea followed by singing in the living room. Christina and Uncle Gordon bonded over their fandom of the Beatles. Uncle Gordon used to be part of a Beatles tribute band when he was in college and he still has his guitar. We sang *Let It Be* and *Hey Jude* and it made the worries I had earlier in the day practically a distant memory.

We ended our time in Douala by visiting my paternal grandparents' home and the neighbouring graves of my grandparents and Uncle Jacobi. We first walked through the house itself. I was curious about how my family would've stayed warm in the house as the marble made the surroundings rather cold. While hot air rises, the concept sometimes goes flat due to the altitude. Thanks to the tropical weather, it never got to freezing levels. We then explored the compound behind the house. My dad said that my grandmother liked gardening, so I bought some flower and herb seeds to plant in the compound. Finally, we spoke to my late paternal grandparents and my uncle. Their graves were just one staircase away from the front door. We had the urge to sing to pay our respects: Christina sang a hymn called *Deo Dicamus Gratias*. Then I sang *The Call* by Regina Spektor. Sarah concluded by singing *Photograph* by Ed Sheeran. Christina and Sarah made remarks about how they were happy to be my friend while I was grateful for them to give me a legacy to live up to. I feel like we had their blessing because not long after Sarah finished her song, the clouds parted, and the sunlight peeked through.

We had lunch at a local restaurant and the mountain fog started building back up again. By the time we started on our way back to Yaoundé, The fog and clouds turned into a torrential downpour. The Douala streets were pretty jammed with cars. One wrong move and the truck could've slammed into any of the other vehicles or a random ramp. All of this felt like a setup towards an epic action film. Mr. Gilbert was honking to try and gain some space. Then he noticed a white military truck with yellow lights, and he was able to follow right behind it. It was like they were working in tandem to get a clear path across the jam to get to the highway - a pretty epic way to get back to Yaoundé.

It was Christina's last day in Cameroon as she had a trip to Beatlesfest in Chicago followed by her move to Los Angeles. We celebrated my birthday a few days early by having dinner at the Hilton. The Prime Minister wanted us to visit together that same evening one last time. We all dressed up to the nines; I wore my favourite one-shoulder purple dress with matching lipstick and hair flower. Christina lent me one of her shawls to ensure I maintained some modesty in the office. Christina wore her pink evening dress with silver accessories – I recognized it from when we went to my brother's wedding and my nephew's baptism. Sarah went for more of a suit-like direction: she wore a purple shirt, white pants, her Harley Quinn Converse, and a black hat she fancied. She completed the look with a pair of sunglasses – it really tied the look together and I could tell that this was the most confident and comfortable she felt outfit-wise. Mom went the complimentary route with a red dress.

Since it was in the evening and we had enough time during the day to rest and recover from our long journey, I was much more awake this time compared to the first. We chatted a lot about history, movies, and our experiences in Cameroon so far. We described our experiences in Oku and Bamenda since the former was his hometown. I was able to ask questions about whether he was still in touch with any of the people we knew in Canada during his ambassador days. I also got a chance to talk about my education, my artistic dreams, and what I would like to do next in my career.

In 2016, I was close to graduation, and I was starting to figure out what I wanted to do after my undergraduate education was over. I bet my younger self would be astounded by where I am now. I've recently graduated from a master's program in one of the best universities in the country in a field that's always been present in my life – theology. Of course, I didn't want to limit myself to theology as it isn't my entire life. I have my artistic pursuits as well with my painting, singing, photography, acting, and writing. Granted, the last thing I expected to be my debut piece was a travel memoir; I had always imagined my first book to be a poetry book, a comic, or a fiction novel. But as many have taught me – from my parents to my family: blood and by choice, you have to start somewhere. Where you are and where you're going to be can feel distant but it's closer than you think. All you need to do is take the first steps.

After we announced our plans for the rest of our evening and the trip, we did one last performance for the prime minister. He invited us to watch his motorcade leave the office that evening. We met with a few more ministers in the office before going back to our Jeep with Mr. Gilbert. We then watched as the motorcycles and the Prime Minister's car pulled out of the secret driveway before speeding off into the night. It was yet another cinematic moment of our trip that I doubt any of us would forget.

The Hilton was right next to the office so the drive was thankfully short. The car was greeted by 3 security officers who did an inspection of the car. My French was rather elementary but one sentence I managed to understand was that there were no guns in the car. It was rather surprising as the trunk looked empty. Yet upon closer inspection, it's easy to see how various modes of hidden security could be implemented. After that inspection, we entered the hotel and proceeded to the buffet. My mom ensured that the buffet was allergen-free, so we enjoyed our dinner to our hearts' content. The food looked like something out of a museum. The desserts and cold cuts were arranged in a neat and artistic fashion. If not for our hunger, we wouldn't have ruined the display. I had wine and Perrier for my refreshment. Christina and Sarah then sang me a birthday song from the Beatles. It was a wonderful surprise. Besides my birthday in Chicago in 2015, I felt an overwhelming sense of love on this occasion. We also sang a song for Mr. Gilbert out of gratitude for taking us everywhere safely and his birthday would happen not long after all of us came back to the States. We then went back to our apartment after finishing our desserts.

Christina really enjoyed our company and wished she didn't have to leave so soon. She Skyped some friends and her parents. She packed all of her things and did her last journal entries. But we didn't want the fun to end. We ended up playing games with the Oreos we brought; one which I remember was the equivalent of the romantic daisy game (loves-me, loves-me-not) where the cream side was who we ended up with, looking up fanfic and *Star Wars* memes, and watching *Don Juan de Marco*. We ended up falling asleep together on my bed after we finished the film.

We went to the Yaounde Nsimalen Airport and said our goodbyes. And so, our trio turned into a duo.

It was a quiet ride back to the apartment as we really felt Christina's absence. I didn't know whether to cry or sleep. I knew Christina was going to have a good time in Beatlesfest and she would be fine in LA. Even with this knowledge, it still felt lonely not having her nearby. Even though I enjoy travel and I've had a lot of friendships that have managed to survive despite continental divides, distance is still a difficult aspect for me to deal with. If it's not funds and transportation, it certainly is the lack of contact and quality time. But I also knew that this wasn't the end of our relationship; this trip, if anything, made our connection that much stronger. We all became like sisters because of it. So, no matter how long it takes for us to reunite – be it a month or a year (or in the case of the pandemic, almost two) – we know we have each other's backs.

Auntie Rachel and Mom noticed the tension, and so they tried to cut through it with some humour and comfort – "at least you'll be able to eat some pineapple now!" It did help release the tension. Mom bought some fresh coconut for us to snack on and possibly drink the water. We eventually forgot about the latter as we went back to Yaoundé a couple of days later. But when we got back to the apartment, we rested in our respective beds. Sarah and I talked about whether either of us would go solo now that we had the space. But we decided to stay together; we got so used to each other's company that we felt like splitting up was pointless. Sarah then introduced me to Aziz Ansari, an Indian American comedian best known for the Netflix series *Master of None*. I had watched a few episodes of it since he was featured on NPR talking about Asian representation in Hollywood. One episode in the first season overtly addressed the stereotypes Asian American actors often have to combat during the audition process, specifically the accent. We watched a recording of his stand-up special in Madison Square Garden. While humour is a hard thing for me to get into, let alone produce in my own life, watching him was a breath of fresh air in the immense seriousness I had taken in my life so far. It also provided me the comfort of the times when I more often don't feel like I'm fitting in.

Between being the child of immigrants, a woman, an intellectual, a nerd, and Black in America, there are so many times where I've felt like I had to prove myself, to carve out a space for myself, to demonstrate that I care and have respect, I'm good enough, and I do belong in a place. Cameroon was a homecoming in the sense that I could see where my parents came from, what they left behind, and what they gained through switching places and, in turn, having me. Of course, it doesn't necessarily mean that it was a good fit either – there are some things that I would not be able to settle with, such as total deference to elders, or near total domestication after marriage and kids. I may also be looked upon as the spoiled, disobedient kid because I leap into a situation a few minutes later rather than the first millisecond or the accent I speak with. There have even been times when I was considered arrogant because of the passport I carry and looked ridiculous at attempting to speak French with a horrid Anglo-American accent despite it being a wonderful opportunity to practice. But for those who took the time to know or accommodate me, especially in times when I felt more like a stranger than family, they gave me the chance to relax, and in turn, I could be me and feel okay that this invisible mess is okay to just be.

We slept in another day to give ourselves enough energy to go back to Douala for my 24th birthday and visit the Cardinal again. Mr. Gilbert stopped by the apartment. He recommended we go for a night-time drive around the city and get some street food before we leave. That brought us back into the exploring mood. We wore our most casual and comfortable clothes before setting off in the night-time Yaoundé streets. With the peril we experienced at arrival far behind us, I found it easier to pay attention to what they had to offer.

With the exception of major intersections, there was a lack of signals on the roads. Driving in Cameroon was a test of every skill possible – from reflexes and observation, to control and signalling. The lack of signals actually made for a much better controlled road as it was more dependent on the situation rather than legality or avoiding fines. Traffic tended to be much higher as well, so what would work in a western city would not work in an African metropolis. The side streets were filled with nightclubs and cafés where people could talk in the open air for hours on end. Unlike the commercialized streets in the US, these places sometimes had no names, known only by their reputation, coloured lights, and mass crowds that darted in and out. Speed was nowhere to be found here – just the ease of the mountainside and the availability of food, drink, and company after a long and hard day. This was true even in the upper districts where we saw the sole Chinese establishment in

# ANCESTRAL HOMECOMING

the area with only a marquee and a pagoda-like structure hinting at the contents inside. Eventually, I'd have a small taste of that life when we returned to Bamenda. But for that one city ride, it was only a possibility.

Mr. Gilbert stopped at one corner where there was a man grilling some fish and chicken. The char and spices could be smelled even within the closed windows. Inside the building, there were more delicious wares to accompany our grilled fare. We came back with grilled fish and chicken fresh from the coals, as well as some fried potatoes, fried plantains, and some boiled cassava, all accompanied with a variety of peppery sauces. It was a simple and delicious dinner, and it felt like Yaoundé's nightlife was giving me a small hug, reassuring me that the rest of the trip would be okay. Early the next morning, with bags full of croissants and cups full of hot beverages, we set off back to Douala to see the Cardinal once again.

We returned to Douala a day before my actual birthday and met up with Aunt Vicky at the Cardinal's residence. I knew about her through letters, emails, and packages my dad would send to her. But this was our first time interacting in person. The family resemblance was uncanny. Face-wise she reminded me of Auntie Marie - one of Aunt Vicky and Dad's siblings and the aunt I've often been mistaken for whenever I go to family outings. Aunt Vicky had a gentle voice and took me in as if we had seen each other for years rather than the one day we had seen each other.

We watched some of the Summer Olympics in Rio de Janeiro. We tuned into the women's basketball game, and it happened to be Team USA and one of my high school friends, Elena Delledonne, was part of the roster that day. I played a game of my own in the background – an old city builder and strategy game called *Stronghold*. After seeing Team USA's victory and just barely

65

clinching my own, Chef David took Sarah and me to the local bakery to pick up a birthday cake from a local bakery.

The sweet smells of fresh baked goods reached through the car. I was so tempted to get the doughnuts on display – they had various flavours of creams and custards inside. But as we were on a tight budget, I kept it simple to a light vanilla cake with a thin layer of chocolate ganache filled with a decadent vanilla cream and a biscuit with 'Joyeux Anniversaire' written at the top. My mom brought special candles with coloured flames to top it off with. I later discovered the reason why my mother gave me so many francs was because she wanted me to treat myself to anything in the bakery. But she liked the cake I had chosen, and we ate the most of it that day and brought the rest back with us to Yaoundé.

\*\*\*

The next few days feel like a blurry montage of activities. We stayed in Yaoundé for a day and visited Auntie Balki and her family. Sarah and I were relaxing in the living room playing with Auntie's cat - a super tiny calico-like creature who was more into playing than being petted. In the background was a rather snowy but distinguishable broadcast of CNN, showing a town hall led by Donald Trump where there was a coordinated set of walkouts. The election was months away and the possibility of his election felt practically impossible. This is an aspect of the trip that still feels the most surreal to me looking back on it. Maybe it was my naivete of being in my 20s or being far, far away from the situation in the US. But the energetic distinction between Cameroon and the US couldn't have felt blurrier at that moment.

The next day, we rode all the way back to Bamenda for my

twin cousin's wedding and visited my grandpa between heavy rainstorms and surgery recovery. We also had many late-night visits by cousins and many older relatives at the family compound, and we went to a couple of nightclubs. Mom, Sarah, and I then visited a king from the kingdom next door through a series of interesting coincidences.

During one of our nightclub visits, Sarah and I saw a group of people sitting in the VIP section, which was empty for most of our visits. I tried not to think too much of it as we were dancing to the various mixes the DJ was pulling up that night. I was sucked into the waves of Motown and Afrobeats for hours until the fatigue from the dancing and wedding caught up to me and we went to our room to rest. We checked out the next day and Sarah and I were the last ones to leave the room after making sure we took everything. A well-dressed man stepped into the elevator just as we were going to go down. To wake myself up and get some French practice, I conversed with him with what I remembered. Through our conversation, I learned that he was also checking out, and he was the one in the VIP section of the nightclub as he remembered us from the night before. I wished him a good day before meeting up with my mother and Auntie Rachel in the lobby. Mom asked me who it was I was talking to, and I explained what I learned. She went straight to his breakfast table; it turned out he was a king from a neighbouring kingdom and Mom recognised him from a documentary. He invited us to come to his palace for lunch and a discussion, and we took him up on his offer the next day. Thankfully, I used the more formal form of speech - something I still do no matter what language I learn and speak. You never know who you're speaking with until they tell you their story!

Finally, we spent a few days in a 4-star hotel in Yaoundé. It was one Mom enjoyed during her previous visit and we luxuriated in its comforts before flying back the exact same path we came in. It was hard not to cry during the first leg of our flight back because it really cemented that the trip was really over. But I came away with an expanded worldview, more nuance in my personal identity, and deep relationships and memories that'll last a lifetime. Writing this story brings a lot of these stories back to the forefront in my mind and it brings me hope and excitement for the adventures to come in my life and my friends and family's lives.

\*\*\*

We did so much in a day that, as well-intentioned as I was in bringing my journal, I didn't have the energy to write full entries; the most I could do was write basic highlights of the days on index cards I brought with me. Thankfully, I also took a lot of videos and photos, so this narrative is the closest I have gotten to proper journal entries of the entire event. I hope this, along with my friends' and my mother's narratives, have given this trip enough justice to anyone who decides to read these pages.

I apologise for any flaws, misconceptions, forgotten facts, people, memories, or offences I may have incurred during its creation, as it's hard to assess the impact of a story until after its completion. This also was written in my 20s during the thick of the COVID-19 lockdown and my graduate school program. Even at that, there are always things we're ahead of the curve, and others where we may be outdated, and I hope to take the time to compensate for the latter in future works.

I thank all of my friends, family, and God for all of the support I have received from start to finish. I also thank you, the reader, for taking the time to hear our stories, and I wish you the best that life has to offer.

**Matanda Wawa Mondoa** recently graduated from Harvard University with a master's degree in world religions. She's excited to get back to travelling, art, and making videos for her YouTube and Twitch channels.

## CHAPTER THREE

# SARAH

## THE GRAND TOUR

Preparations were quick as soon as we bought the idea of my going to Cameroon with the Mondoas. Before we knew it, take off was the next day. So, the night before we headed for the airport, we went to church. The blessings from a priest and his congregation were our goal. However, not much was clear to me since I am not Catholic. This was the first time I had been blessed and the first trip I was taking in which anyone considered it necessary to be blessed before going on it. I couldn't place the requirement on the idea of a flight since it was not my first time on a plane.

The other side of the church service was that we were also there to perform our *Seasons of Love* for the congregation. It's a beautiful song from the 1996 Broadway musical RENT by Jonathan Larson and starts with "525600 minutes" (the number of minutes in an ordinary year). The year is to be measured:

In daylights,
In sunsets,
In midnights,
In cups of coffee,

In inches, in miles, in laughter, in strife…
It serialises questions on how to measure a year in a life:
How about love? How about love? How about love?
Measure in love… Seasons of love… Seasons of love
If it is about measuring the life of a woman or man, it proposes:
In truth that she learned
Or in times that she cried
In bridges he burned
Or the way that she died

It's time to sing our thought
The story never ends.
Let's celebrate, remember a year in a life
Of friends
The song ends with the command to
Remember the love…
(Sing out, give out, measure your life
In loooooove…!)
Seasons of love…
Seasons of love…
© Universal Music Corp, Finster & Lucy Music Ltd. Co.

The combination of the brisk melodiousness and lyrics with the knowledge that it was a RENT production iced the cake of my inner *schadenfreude*.

The entire trip comes in broken pieces of memory to me. I do remember that we took lots of photos that were tiresome then, but became props of memory later.

From the pictures, for instance, I remember wearing a green dress shirt and black pants with a pair of white sneakers. I recall, too, that the other four weren't, like me, as worried about losing their dress shoes in the shuffle of the eventful times we had.

I was nervous and ought to be, especially as I eventually 'lost' my pair of Harley Quinn Converse. It finally revealed that they were not lost, even if we were once confident that they were. They had simply been placed in a different bag to distribute weight. In the flurry and comixing or commingling of our personal utilities, we all forgot that detail when we began unpacking the bags later.

We were Auntie Rachel, Auntie Ambrosia or simply "Auntie," and Christina (in the same photo outside the church, she threw her hands in the air as if she didn't care), then Matanda.

Father Roger and the other person I didn't know also joined us for a picture. I hardly even knew Father Roger at this point, but he comes through as someone with a great sense of humour.

After the mass and pictures, we all returned to Matanda's house for dinner. It was as delicious as I've come to expect at the Mondoa residence. The evening was enhanced by the many family friends and relatives who stopped by, as well as the conversation and pleasantries. My parents weren't able to make it, though. God knows they helped me make it this far.

\*\*\*

The next morning's hustle and bustle was simply chaotic, the chaos of managing the multiple little concerns of the trip. For example, I remember a slight issue fitting everyone's luggage into the car, which required more concentrated calculation than I would otherwise have granted. Well, even chaos has an end and eventually, we were airport bound. "Uncle," as we referred to Dr Mondoa, dropped us off at the JFK airport, but he wasn't flying with us.

I packed the least in terms of weight and volume. However, because one of the suitcases was filled with non-perishable food for all of us, we were all left with overfilled luggage. My own hands were worse than overloaded because, anticipating the AC on the airplane, I wore a black suit. For the moment, I toted the jacket in my arms, not knowing where else to put it. This added to my embarrassment when our luggage exceeded the protocol limit at check-in.

Then, seated by the aisle, I kept staring at the window, which attracted the attention of my fellow passenger (a stranger). It was an old habit I found difficult to drop. I watched the window to convince myself of the possibility of jumping out for survival. But this was only at the take-off point when my body had to adjust to its fright of the turbulent airlift.

I'm fine once the plane gets high enough, but before then, I am stressed. The stranger whose attention I attracted was very kind. She also spoke French, which mildly embarrassed me that I hadn't learned any substantial French despite the several months' notice. I was uncomfortable with the fact that we were en route to Cameroon, where I was going to need some French. Nonetheless, a little later, I was somewhat mollified that I could read some French, thanks to some Spanish knowledge.

Airborne, I am determined not to sleep much on the flight and try adjusting to the new time zone. This plan is thwarted by the lights going off somewhere over the Atlantic, which brings up my poor handling of boredom.

We arrived at the Brussels airport mid-morning and, with gusto, skipped out for Belgian waffles and chocolates. It is the lone exercise worth mentioning here while we wait for our next flight. However, food allergy complicates this venture, forcing us to go a long way to avoid inducing a reaction.

We are soon on our next flight, heading straight from Brussels to Douala. We get lunch on the plane like we previously got dinner and breakfast, and I am at a loss as to whether this extra service is part of the niceties of any flight or just something for an international flight. I while away the flight time reading a *Star Wars* novel. My engaging interest in this exercise makes me wonder why I didn't pack more books.

Then we are flying over the Sahara. The transition from the abstract knowledge of its being the world's largest desert to the actual experience is worlds apart. It is unlike anything I have seen previously; I was unprepared for the tan and brown ocean below. This perhaps explains why I was fully awake right to Douala.

At Douala, we waited on the plane during the transfer to Yaoundé. It is the shortest flight I have been on since the Chicago-Minneapolis layover.

Christina puts on some Beatles music, but the view of the Wouri River catches our attention and weaves itself into our conversation. Auntie Rachel tells us how the Portuguese named the country after this river, where they found a lot of prawns, from the river of prawns, which in Portuguese is Rio dos camarões, the name Cameroon was born. Looking at it, I can see why.

A loose comment from Auntie about us celebrating Matanda's birthday confuses me as I imagine the day was actually Matanda's birthday.

While waiting for the other passengers to get off, Christina and I start dancing in the aisle. Christina has that effect on people. She got a joke offer of marriage from a mother in the market for her son. We learn from Auntie's explanation that the woman was complimenting Christina. It made sense to think that someone has to have a good enough impression of you to invite you to join their family.

We got off the plane. The airport looks a little smaller. We search and get someone to help us with the luggage. Once we exit the airport, two gentlemen welcome us. They have come in two vehicles and I assume they are relatives or friends of the family. One of them is Uncle Louis. We get into two different cars, a splitting of the team, which makes the tourist in me somewhat nervous even though I'm there with Christina, Matanda, and the gentleman driving. Several things play up with my nervousness. I guess it has something to do with the darkness, some disorientation or startling because it's about 7 p.m. local time. Also, it is cooler than I expected, which does not quite click with the fact that we are on the equator.

I was hardly out of my tenseness before things got worse. We hit a pothole that is wide and deep enough to require towing help, which doesn't seem so available. So, my anxiety inflates into alarm. What thoughts spin in my head are a whorl. Centrally, I think, I just want to get to where we're going to catch up on lost sleep. It is not a long wait before another car pulls up, which we get into instead. The coordination is not within my competence to grasp.

It is a relief that we get there not too long after. It's a nice place - kitchen, dining room, living room, multiple bathrooms, multiple bedrooms, lights, tiled floors, windows - cool. The little snag is that there aren't enough beds for all five of us. But we have mattresses and bed sheets aplenty. We do not have mosquito nets for the night, though. So, we spritz ourselves with bug spray and lie down to sleep, Matanda and I sharing a room.

Just as sweet Morpheus approaches, I hear the tell-tale whine of a mosquito. Could we ignore them? No, not when they whine so close to the ears, and you know they are carriers of deadly diseases, including malaria. We rise to the situation and try everything. Swatting (Matanda is much better at this), more spraying, ignoring them, and even relocation (on my part) to the living room. My relocation is futile, for it is too chilly for comfort. At some point after midnight, we discovered the cause of our plight: the adjacent bathroom's window had been left open, perhaps by a cleaner or a previous tenant. We close the window. We resort to pretending that any remaining blighters weren't there.

It is not the length of sleep we anticipated, for Auntie wakes us up around five the next morning. She is pleased to tell us that the Prime Minister can make time for us to visit him that morning. First, however, we are going to Auntie's alma mater, or so I conjectured. The college was lovely. However, considering how I managed to stick my foot in my mouth while there, the context needs clarification.

We took a taxi for the first few days. The streets in the capital differed by pavement, depending upon traffic. More major roads matched my expectations; the rest were packed dirt. I was oddly taken by the colour, which was more red than expected. Little room was wasted on parking lots or unnecessary sidewalks. Most remarkable, to me at least, was the lack of traffic lights or signs I could discern. As it turns out, however, drivers are perfectly capable of functioning without them, provided that they drive carefully (i.e., slowly) and that they communicate with each other (i.e., honk). The strong scent of car fuel is unmistakable, and there is nothing romantic about it. However, the buildings were as tall as I would have expected in a capital city and in the distance, we could see the undulating hills of the country. There was a lot of foot traffic, sometimes in the intersections, selling wares, but much more frequently on the side of the road.

What struck me more during the commute was the sheer

variety in appearances. Plenty of people were dressed in T-shirts and other clothing I had come to think of as ubiquitous to large cities, but a good number were wearing headdresses and what I would have considered more traditional clothing.

It is in the backdrop of this setting that, with the others, I get to Auntie's alma mater. We sit in a lecture hall with polished wooden desks on a tiered carpet in an amphitheatre. At this point, I managed to miscommunicate this observation to Auntie. She seemed to think I thought the T-shirts remarkable rather than the reverse. I was wrong either way, but I would like to be side-eyed for the right reasons. Given the circumstances, and putting it mildly, it was ironic. Eventually, we had to leave the hall to be on time for the other rendezvous.

We head straight to the Prime Minister's office, a building set on a hill and close to a hotel. It has a spectacular view of the rest of the city. We waited in a lovely lobby with a thick red carpet. It wasn't a long wait, for we were soon invited to see Prime Minister Philemon Yang.

It turns out Auntie had spoken to him before, a detail I only learned about a week later. In the sleep-deprived haze I was in, I remember very little about the conversation. Apart from the introductions, I can recall some dark humour about the 2016 presidential campaign in the US and automobiles—their history and use in both the US and Cameroon. I remember thinking he and my father would get on well if the topic didn't turn to politics.

Befuddled by sleep, I felt lucky to be wearing sunglasses that hid my drooping eyes from betraying what might appear like a lack of interest. At the very end of the visit, we sang Glee's version of Journey's *Don't Stop Believin'*. We hoped that our performance would appeal to our august audience and serve as a form of friendly gift brought along for the visit.

The idea of performance was born out of two different threads. First, Christina is a professional singer, Matanda is a regular chorister for her church choir, and I sang until my second year of college. The second thread is more traditional. A performance is a way of showing gratitude to your host, which seemed appropriate. Christina, bless her, helped us choose songs (singles, duets, and trios) and even outfits for likely occasions.

When we got back to the apartment, I could not imagine the magnitude of what we were doing or what was happening around us. I hit the mattress and passed out for quite a few hours.

\*\*\*

I honestly can't recall if the trip to the museum was the next day. We took a taxi, and Auntie told the driver to pick us up at a prearranged time. We walked up the long driveway to the National Museum—a beautiful white building that once served as the Presidential Mansion. Its central structure dates back to the 1930s. Wings were added to this main structure in the 1960s, and the whole structure served as the presidency until the Unity Palace was constructed to serve as the new presidency.

We didn't have to step inside to start seeing the art. Outside the building were several metal statues, probably made of bronze. I most remember the spiders flanking the stairs and a female elder in front of which we took several pictures on our way out.

Identification was one requirement before one was allowed inside the museum. Electronic or other storage gadgets were not allowed, and no pictures were allowed to be taken inside either. I had not thought to take my passport from my luggage because it could be stolen. The museum authorities were kind enough to let me in any way. It has been about four years since, and sans photographic cues, I still recall a few things about that first visit.

I remember we sang the National Anthem as our "thank you" song, an odd choice, given that the 2016 US presidential campaign was on. I wasn't feeling especially patriotic. However, we had just learned the Cameroonian national anthem, so it was appropriate enough. I remember the rooms and rooms of photos, mostly of people crucial to Cameroon's independence from Britain and France. While we visited the rooms, I think most of my time was spent looking at Auntie than at the photos. She kept telling stories about people in the photos, a continuous flow of informative material.

I learned that Cameroon had been a one-party state, which was quite a surprise, for I considered even two parties too few. Perhaps this was obvious from my facial expression because we were told the rationale: the one-party narrative was construed to mean greater national unity while at the same time recognising the diversities even within the party. The logic synced with the local fact that the country comprised many semi-autonomous kingdoms. Given the eventualities of the years that followed and the happenings since 2017 and up to this moment, the clarification about diversity and the need for greater unity was an important distinction.

Speaking of the kingdoms, there was a room with three-dimensional figures (dioramas) of the different styles of architecture specific to the various kingdoms. However, there was an entire wing dedicated to modern art. It was a massive feast for the eyes, and we could hardly do justice given the time we had left. We left as it was getting dark, although the entire lower floor was still lit.

***

Concentrating on visited spots without the food component leaves out a major factor. For breakfast, we usually had cereal with milk powder and water. These had all been packed well ahead of time. On a particularly good morning, we had pastries from a local bakery or puff-puff, a type of fried dough. Fried bread or puff-puff was relatively constant. Lunch and dinner were when we would be spoiled. Some recurring dishes included rice overladen with chicken, beef stew, or seasoned beans, fish off the bone, fried plantains, better known as "dodo" and "fufu" or yam with bitter leaf or seasoned vegetables.

Bananas were quite a stir when we saw them. They were a vibrant shade of yellow that made American bananas look like milk. I remembered my friend Nicki, who was in agribusiness, telling me about monocultures in American agriculture.

The food was very filling. Auntie hypothesised this was because they had not needed to be processed in any way. We could get more for less.

As for drinkables, anything we drank that wasn't tea or coffee came from a bottle. I have never been a big soda person, but I drank a lot of Fanta that month. We also drank a lot of tea.

\*\*\*

We went to church on Sunday, something I hadn't done for some time. It was not like other services I had been to and was primarily in French, which struck me as fair since we were in a country where the two official languages are French and English. So, the service had me dredging up all I remembered on church etiquette to avoid being visibly bored during the relatively long service. The boredom did not last as long as one might expect, even though I was neither following the scripture readings nor the homily. I noted that one advantage of Catholicism was that you can follow the Mass format anywhere in the world. I did "my best" with the singing, though Auntie helped immensely in that direction. The offering was the most exciting part, given its novelty vis-à-vis what I was used to - a basket being passed up and down the pews. Here, accompanied by music, we filed up and placed the offering just as if you were going up for Communion. Now, too, the music was much livelier. People, myself included, practically danced on their way up.

*  *  *

Church over, I think it was the same day we visited the Cameroon Radio Television (CRTV), the equivalent of our Public Broadcasting Service (PBS). There, we got a tour from the director, which was quite a thrill, but this is where the bilingual aspect began to sink in for me. Going to one of the offices, we could see people editing film and audio on their computers right before us. We also went to one of the consoles that were empty of people. The furniture was there, and they graciously allowed us to ham it up.

While the feast of the eyes and ears went on, I had the misfortune that my heels were not as comfortable as I had thought when I purchased them; walking was unpleasant. That was one gritty thing I had to endure because it was not as if I could rectify the situation and take off the footwear at will.

*  *  *

The meltdown I had later that day was a more memorable crisis than ill-fitting shoes. What happened was that we were all tired, which was due to the amount of singing and pacing at CRTV. I was not the most anxious person in the lot, but that was due to an atypically lackadaisical attitude I had adopted. For one thing, I didn't know the people around me much, and I wasn't a professional in singing performance. So, if they held it against me for going off-pitch, that wasn't fair by my reckoning, and I wouldn't have to live with it. It was a shame on them, I held, given how little advance notice or prep we got. The information for specific performances was abrupt, and I clarified that to someone more unsettled by this.

Auntie got to know; how, I don't know because, after the fact, it never seemed prudent to ask. Based on the confrontation or my sympathetic reaction, she approached us, probably feeling frustrated by it. She seemed hurt, indicating her feeling that we had been going behind her back unnecessarily, as we could frankly have told her that we didn't want to sing.

This baffled me for multiple reasons. In the first place, my understanding of the concept of venting dictated that you did not go to the source of your frustration unless the situation actually warranted it. I had never felt so aggrieved that I found it necessary not to sing. So, I had no desire to cease singing altogether, and the lack of, or the short notice, was only a minor irritation for which I had expressed sympathy. But Auntie was an authority figure, which compounded matters a little.

Besides, since this was brought up, it was not a matter of trusting or not trusting a guardian who ensured no harm befell you when travelling. Trusting them with one's squishy emotions was a different ball game altogether. I wasn't doubting Auntie on her guardianship, which would have been assuming that she lacked basic decency. At this point, Auntie's reaction instead ruffled and confused me. Pointedly, I did not know Auntie very well at this point, which has since changed. However, even today, I would say we have very different approaches to this sort of situation, which, of course, is due to cultural and temperamental differences.

One might think that with all these reasons for being baffled, that past me would have been more confused than anything else. However, I do not always behave rationally in stressful situations, and this is not an open confession since it is something those who know me a little more can hardly miss. For instance, in elementary school, I remember an incident during one of our bathroom breaks when I assumed it was my fault that the class was being lectured on making noise in the bathroom just because I was one of three girls in the bathroom at the time, and happened to drop something on the floor. However, that was because the other two girls and what they had been doing had slipped my mind entirely. On that occasion, I cried, and that was really for no reason at all.

But here, I held myself together until Auntie left the room. Then I burst into tears and apologised for upsetting Auntie and started apologising for crying. Of course, apologising for everything is not an attractive quality - a thing one of my co-workers had to remind me of back in 2015. God bless Matanda and Christina. They handled my outburst like champs, and the next day, we were leaving Yaoundé, destination - Matanda's grandparents in Ndop.

Unlike the first morning in Yaoundé after a late-night battle with mosquitoes, getting up early for the Ndop trip was not challenging.

The trip had various attractions, and we had an offer from a family friend - a chauffeur, Mr Gilbert, who would drive us to any destination of our choice within the country. While this was money-saving for us, the added benefit for Mr Gilbert was that he could visit his family in Oku. The human component is that he was excellent company and quite a savvy driver. Besides, we also had the advantage of having a white license plate, the government one. License plates are colour-coded, including orange for civilians and white for government officials.

City traffic was heavy until we exited the city, which offered an exquisite illustration of funnelling contributing to traffic density. But, out of the city, we had a day ahead of driving. Necessarily, we had a few stops along the way.

The first stop I remember was when we pulled over on the side of the road. Auntie wanted to show us something. We walked down a trail, admiring some crop flowers, including plantains. We then emerged on a bank from which we could view a waterfall, and this was splendid. The scenery that spread before us all through the journey was captivating.

We glided, sandwiched by forests, hills, and giant palm trees that I would sooner associate with the beaches of Florida, but we were definitely not at sea level. A quick look at the ground showed that the soil was typically mostly red and quite different from the soil back home. This made my nerd parts happy and excited. The combination of piquing varieties of vegetation, soil colours, flat country and hilly undulations justified what I later learned about Cameroon being sometimes referred to as "Africa in miniature."

The ride was long, though, and we naturally needed to stop at one point in a little town where the main road comprised the main street. Primarily, we stopped to use the facilities, which offered me the need to be authentic without being crass about it. Depending on where you were, the plumbing may or may not accommodate flushing. In this little town, it did not. But the solution was straightforward - you took a bucket of water and poured it in when you were done. It was that simple and essentially performed the same role.

I went in and squatted, but I was paranoid more than anything else, for sitting was an option. There were flies, many indeed. It was, of course, a public restroom. It opened to the outdoors like any beach bathroom you've ever been in. This facility served us well.

We also stopped at a gas station at one point, which was a relief, given that the road got bumpier, the tar broken or sometimes completely scraped off, and the terrain really rugged. This was especially noticed as we headed towards more rural areas. It was getting darker, too, and more difficult to orient ourselves and our movement relative to our surroundings. However, the driver seemed to know exactly where we were, where and how we were getting to our destination. The disorientation had its toll on me as I started getting carsick. Thank God we were only about an hour from our destination and eventually arrived there. But before I talk about Ndop, a few observations that do not fit neatly into dates need to be mentioned.

We snacked a lot of food back there, especially on puff-puff, as fried dough was called. I think fried dough is a universal constant. But our conversation was mostly not about local realities but rather about media (TV shows, movies, books), as two out of the three of us are nerds. This was particularly true in the car, where we hardly used our phones. At those moments, my little brain gremlins of story plots, original as well as derivative, jumped to the fore to play freely. I had to borrow so many notecards from Matanda, dear Lord, to write them down to be able to remember them.

I should pause here to reflect on this divergence, which

differs from hooking unto the gritty present. Indeed, it hardly seems to be. While the weather and other hard and palpable experiences intruded on us, we chose to float on the clouds of TVs, movies, and books. As an escapist, I should consider shifting from the concrete experience to the realistic present. Yet, a nudge behind my mind asks: What is the realistic present if not what you choose to be in your focus? For the physical may pique and prod, giving the impression of being the real, but really, focus is what is really real, odd as it sounds. What you focus on becomes your reality, I have heard it said.

Besides French, Creole (from the linguistic standpoint), referred to as "Pidgin", was commonly used. I was not about to start telling them why it was Creole rather than pidgin, but I grew better at it. But it is linguistically a Creole being a fully developed language. "Pidgin" refers to a less developed language used to navigate different language backgrounds. It certainly is not "bad" English. Did I say I got better at it? I can't speak it to save my life. However, I started laughing at a punchline they weren't expecting me to be listening to, let alone understand. So, I suppose I was getting better at it! It was nice.

Now, back to Ndop, we got there when it was dark. It is located in the North West Region of Cameroon. A good thing my dad didn't know we were going there, or he might not have let me. I didn't keep it from him on purpose, though. What he did know was that we were going to Yaoundé and Douala. Ndop, for him, would have suggested somewhere too close to Nigeria, where Boko Haram was then making headlines. Being a retired military man, my dad checked government websites when my going to Cameroon came up. When he hesitated, I told him he had every right to refuse to pay, but my dad is a softie. However, if safety was his concern, he had to call Mrs Mondoa first. For her part, my mom was so excited that I was travelling. Not so my sister, who was convinced that I was surely going to do something stupid and contract a disease on the trip.

None of these home concerns seem related to where we now were - Ndop. Grandma's "house," as it was referred to, actually consisted of a few buildings. There was a kitchen, as well as a house for a great-aunt. She was adorable and quite blind. The atmosphere was unmistakably rural, with goats, chickens, tall palm trees and various field crops. Outside stood a rain barrel to catch fresh water. When it rained, it poured, and we stood on the porch to watch and collect it in buckets.

Grandma's main house had a kitchen, a living room, a few bathrooms, and bedrooms. In the living room was a TV set and several valuables from Grandfather's long career as a manager. The wood carvings and a set of tusks stand out in my memory.

The bathrooms had a sink and a toilet but no running water, and you needed a bucket to bathe. At first, I thought this would be stranger than it ended up being. Before long, I was well-acquainted with the bathroom procedures, mainly due to gynaecological medication backfiring.

Of course, malaria pills could also have contributed. I had to choose between two different types. The side effects were either the risk of an upset stomach or a possible psychotic break if you had a pre-existing mood disorder or anxiety. Those tend to be under-diagnosed, and I didn't like my odds. The Yaoundé experience of mosquitoes was still at the back of my mind; the potential malaria attack was quite an issue.

At grandma's, we each got our bed and accompanying light blue mosquito netting, which I delighted in calling fairy gauze. A handful of rips were detected, mostly tucked under the mattress. I think the tears came from the rough encounter with the rough woodwork of the bed under the mattress. The remaining rips could easily be stopped by stuffing a small piece of cloth. Only one mosquito managed to get at me, and that was a lot later in the trip.

Matanda, Christina, and I didn't contribute much to the household. I'm not sure anyone wanted us to. To this day, I'm not sure if that's because Grandma was a sweetheart or despaired of our cluelessness. She started fussing once when I was carrying a bucket of water from the water barrel, which made it possible that we were just being spoiled.

We did wash dishes and our clothes, scrubbing and rubbing each garment and part till they were clean. There was no washing machine. Something I perceive as a minor miscommunication was that Auntie expected me to bathe more often and to re-wear clothes.

Regarding the home interaction, Grandpa was unfortunately quite ill and in the hospital a good deal while we visited. I had difficulty understanding him when he talked, so I didn't interact with him much; I also figured he needed the rest. Now that he is dearly departed, I regret being less interactive with him then.

In the house was an adorable preteen named Daryl, whom we all enjoyed spoiling. There were other children, but he was the most talkative of the bunch. We showed him Zootopia and a few other movies on our laptops; we played a few games on the laptops, too. Matanda set up a hotspot so we could keep using the Internet, but it was rather patchy.

While in Ndop, we visited a palace. It was a shocker, for I learned that one of my best friends was related to a king. Matanda was of royal blood, which is why we visited the palace and were allowed into some of the palace sections in Cameroon.

While I have not been inside Buckingham Palace, only

outside of it, I can say this palace was smaller. Instead, it vaguely reminded me of a villa. The architecture was beautiful, particularly the pillars, and I am partial to that colour.

We met His Majesty, and he hugged all three of us, which we did not expect. He was very hospitable and offered us drinks. In turn, we sang a bit, I remember. Our singing indicated our goodbye. So, we were soon bound for Oku.

\*\*\*

After Ndop, we went to Oku. On the way, we visited a tea factory and took pictures of the fields. Alex, my more tea-savvy friend, was not there, but it was exciting nonetheless, and we were encouraged to collect a few tea leaves for the future.

Nearby was a beautiful blue mosque, from where I remember hearing the sounds of the *adhan* from the minaret, the tower on its top. The adhan was a daily call to prayer, one of the five, made by the muezzin. It was loud enough to be heard as we took pictures in the field.

Before exploring the factory properly, we visited the attached zoo, passing droves of large cattle on the walk there. The zoo attractions included ostriches or emus (not sure exactly which), baboons, and chimpanzees. We saw the chimpanzees being fed. They fished out the filling out of the rice cakes they were given in one of many examples of recognisably human behaviour. However, the true jewel for me was the python. I had seen one at Dover, and now I was seeing another. So, I was drawn by familiarity with this one, thousands of kilometres away in Cameroon. To me, she was beauty and grace as she slithered right past my view with gorgeous shimmers.

From the zoo, we went into the factory, thanks to the owner

who did not join us then. We watched the conveyor belts and the complex accomplishment of moving the leaves, shredding them, etc. We stopped to smell the finished product and were informed of the beneficial effects of the flavour itself before we went to the owner's office, who gave us boxes of tea and cloth with the company logo printed on them. I remember Auntie telling him how he could use the shredded powder to create iced tea to sell. It turns out iced tea is much more of an American thing.

The greenery, zoo, and factory combined to make our visit memorable. Unfortunately, it was getting late, and we had to reach our initial destination—Oku.

So, we left the tea estate and headed for Oku, which had steep climbs and descents. Mainly, we had a steep drive up the mountain, with many turns. The cloud cover got thicker as we negotiated the incline until we pulled up in front of a rather nondescript, seemingly unused building. Stray or free-range goats were around.

Either Auntie or Mr Gilbert was in the lead as we descended a flight of steps down the slope into the forest. Germans had built these before being forced away by the British here (and the French in the other regions of the country), who had colonised the area. The steps were steep, but I enjoyed the trip down because I liked hiking. It was so quiet; it was like the middle of nowhere.

Lake Oku is a captivating sight, a crater lake, so serene or rather, quietly majestic and resting or leaning on the surrounding heights as it were that the one bird we saw on its surface stuck out like a sore thumb. The water was so clear, so unruffled, which leagues with what my mother had told me about hiking in the mountains of California and how the water high up is cleaner. Never having been to California, I had only had a point of reference once I was here at the shores of Lake Oku.

We took pictures until the cloud cover that had constantly been skimming the lake's surface threatened to get thicker. On the sides of whispered stories, the lake has myths surrounding it that involve a spirit village. We gathered a few bottles of the mysterious waters as souvenirs and bid goodbye to it as more clouds gathered.

As it was getting late, we opted to stay a night in the local hotel, which did not see much business that night. There, we had dinner that was comprised of chicken prepared by one of the town's lady chefs. Culture shock took its toll on us. We were taken aback and quite alarmed by the presence of chicken intestines, thinking there had been some kitchen error until Auntie assured us that it had been left there intentionally. It had been properly cleaned. The idea was that leaving out a part of the dish's meat would have been considered rude to us. With that explanation, we opted to give it a try. It tasted like undercooked noodles in chicken broth, i.e., simply chewy but definitely good.

Dinner over, we went to our room to sleep. Our room was separate from Auntie and Auntie Rachel's, the hotel being set up in a villa style so that we were roughly across a courtyard from them. There were two beds in our room, as well as a couch. I volunteered to take the couch and regretted my choice later that night, and even unsuccessfully tried to see if Christina, who had gotten the larger bed, could be politely roused to share space. It was cold in the mountains.

We bathed with buckets of heated water set in the shower stall. Afterwards, it began raining, and what a rain it was. Sleets of heavy raindrops slapped against the ground. The huge raindrops were like hailstones. We hadn't experienced rain at Grandma's, so the girls and I were awestruck. We went outside with flashlights to experience the drumming at close quarters. There was enough room in the porches for this. It turned out that Auntie and Auntie Rachel saw our actions from their room.

*　*　*

The excitement of the lake experience, the awesome sleets of night rain and the cold of Oku heights went by and we focused on the next stop, which was going to be the city of Douala. Our link and the focal person there was none other than Christian Cardinal Tumi. Douala was a large city and the economic capital of Cameroon, while Yaoundé was the political capital. Both cities had the same density but differed in the atmosphere of activities and utilities. Yaoundé was hilly, while Douala was sea-level flat, humid and hotter.

On our way to Douala, we stopped at the house of Auntie's friend, a most gracious host. Unfortunately, I was lost to this magnanimous character because of a preoccupation with misplacing my phone. Actually, it was forgotten at the home of our gracious host, who thankfully had it enveloped, and we collected it on our way back. That is how my memory of the visit to Auntie's friend became very sketchy, except for the overall impression of her extraordinary homeliness.

The Cardinal lived next door to a large church house, all within a walled compound. Upon being let in, we saw some dogs at the guard post when we exited the car. They seemed pretty friendly but were definitely keeping an eye on things. A few poultry birds could also be seen in the courtyard from where we were let into an air-conditioned living room. There we waited. We arrived when our host was away. Given the long journey, it was hard to be precise about the arrival time. We waited.

Matanda, Christina and I managed to embarrass ourselves by not rising for his Eminence when he walked in. It did not immediately occur to us to stand up when he entered. Nothing was lost, however, and it was soon dinner time. Not only was the meal delicious, but everyone was warm and friendly. We gave our compliments directly to the chef. The ambience reminded me of a Thanksgiving dinner in my family in the sense that the elders were mainly doing the talking. Of course, they also expressed opinions that I disagreed with, but like most Thanksgivings, it seemed unwise to be contentious. It filtered from the conversation that my friend had been a miracle baby, what with infant health concerns, which occasioned an unusual choice of godparents. Otherwise, the cardinal's abode was cool.

The following day, we drove about fifty kilometres to visit Matanda's father's alma mater, St. Joseph's College Sasse, one of several long row-type buildings. The grounds were largely empty at this time of year, but we did meet the accompanying bishop, for whom I ended up singing "Popular" by Wicked. How it happened can best be explained as the result of a panic impulse. Or, you know that moment when someone is going to raise their hand, so it might as well be you? He seemed to enjoy it, though, which made it not a total loss. For the night, we put up in a nice hotel, but an incident sprang up.

At the hotel, we warned the staff not to serve pineapple, no cross-contamination, we explained, because one of us had a severe food allergy. But pineapple was part of the breakfast buffet, and I got rather indignant on my friend's behalf. She was undoubtedly incensed because of cross-contamination, which resulted in anaphylactic shock. Upon sober thought, it looks as if we had overreacted. There was some back-and-forth about this within our group, but ultimately, we brought it up again, which was taken pretty seriously. Someone got fired. We were shocked by that last part, but we were later told that, given the hotel's clientele, they couldn't afford to take this matter lightly.

We drove from the hotel to visit another family friend. While we were there, I realized that I had managed to ingratiate myself with Auntie. Someone at the table said that we - Matanda and I - were very quiet and well-behaved. Auntie, with all the mirth of an affectionate parent, said that we were not always this quiet and that when we were quiet, we were still thinking. I was touched by this because it showed me that she knew me and she did not prefer my more socially acceptable but less authentic traits.

It was from this home of Auntie's friend that we took a short drive to visit the graves of Uncle's parents. But before leaving, we sang. I drew from my quick repertoire of acapella songs, ending up going with Ed Sheeran's *Wait for Me to Come Home*. By it, I interpreted this trip as a homecoming.

***

Shortly after this, we had to head back to Yaoundé so that Christina could catch her flight. We were in Cameroon for 28 days, but Christina had to get back to the States just after fourteen days for career reasons. As a result, many destinations had been squeezed into the first half of the trip, so the rigorous pacing slowed a bit after her departure.

Before she left, however, we visited the Prime Minister one more time. We were in his office for hours, which meant he indulged us, given the state duties he was supposed to focus on. I can only assume that he enjoyed our company. For my part, I certainly had a better time now that I did not need to contend with the sleep deprivation of the first encounter. I was vigilant this time around and even sang in the lobby, which, in hindsight, may have been a bit much.

We had the opportunity to watch him leave with the pomp of statesmanship. It was quite a spectacle: an escort of guards on motorcycles, a car ahead of his, and two cars following his. The arrangement certainly had a security element, but it looked like state pageantry.

A stone's throw from the Prime Ministry was the Hilton Hotel, where we shifted to celebrate Matanda's birthday, with Mr Gilbert accompanying us. We sang to Matanda this time, *For Good* from *Wicked*, *Happy Birthday*, this trip was really for you. Even then, I still thought her birthday was in July, as I had done on the airplane. Only in 2017 did I get my bearings right.

The next day, we took Christina to the airport. And while we saw her off at the airport, Auntie chased off a man whom I recall as vaguely solicitous but who was raising her alarm bells. I also remember Christina's hair bow, which looked like Minnie Mouse's ears.

Well, we saw her off and, shortly after, headed back to Douala to see the Cardinal again. It seemed like we were establishing a rhythm. We had seen the Prime Minister twice, and now it was the Cardinal we would meet for the second time. However, this time, it was also Matanda's birthday. So, we went to the bakery and got a chocolate cake, and the Cardinal joined us in celebrating. We attended Mass the next morning, and another striking thing happened during the offertory procession. Folks were bringing produce to the altar. I imagined these would prove helpful for the fellowship meal later. However, Matanda and I put our feet in our mouths when we later saw a live chicken in our host's kitchen and thought the meat would be fresher than we had assumed. We were, however, entirely mistaken. Nothing followed from there, but we did heartily enjoy the buffet.

\* \* \*

We were going to leave for Yaoundé, but that couldn't be before several stops. First, we visited a bishop's house and were graciously offered some snacks; I think it was nuts of some sort. Also, while Auntie visited her father in the hospital, Matanda and I visited a farm belonging to a family friend. Granddad had not been well while we were visiting, but he got better by the end of our trip.

The host whose farm we visited had a keyboard on which we did a duet, *A Thousand Miles*. It was not a performance for an audience, just the two of us before our host took us out to the farm to show how it was set up. There were layers built into the hill like a giant staircase, the poultry having enclosures for security and perhaps for better managing the birds. We moved from there, still within the city, to another friend's house. She had a kitten and served us dinner while we watched a TV broadcast of protesters interrupting Donald Trump's 2016 campaign speech.

\* \* \*

Many other recollections get rather woolly, but two stand to memory - a wedding and clubbing. For the wedding, someone came and took our measurements. The day came, and we got the dresses, each of us making a pick of our style, while the cloth mainly remained white, with primarily blue designs. The bride and groom stood out with their white dress and grey suit, respectively, and the church ceremony was orderly. The sanctity of traditional marriage was harped upon. Following the ceremony was a great party, with delicious food and dancing. I botched a singing performance, though. I also noticed that there were gate-crashers. Overall, it was nothing less than a great night.

The wedding party reminds me of Matanda and I going clubbing, although I cannot pin it whether it was before or after the wedding. I remember that we stayed at the hotel the evening before and after the wedding. The club basement of the hotel made it so conducive for us to get going. I forget whose idea led us to decide on it, even though neither of us had clubbed before this day. There had to be a first, and here it was at an international hotel. You can be sure it wouldn't be an open door for all possibilities. Yeah, Auntie made sure she sent Mr Gilbert with us, and I can't blame her, for it was new grounds where only maturity and experience might save us from an unpleasant eventuality. It might even have been Auntie Rachel's idea because she came with us, too. On her part, Auntie graciously told us we would be sleeping in the next morning. But sleeping in for her would only mean going on till 8 a.m.

We went down into the club. Lots of lights, deafening music, and cigarette smoke marked it for what it was. There were drinks, but we elected not to order. Keen observation required concentration and, certainly, sobriety. In any case, clubbing didn't mean we were supposed to go wasting.

The dance floor consisted of big block plastic tiles that lit up in different colours. Older gentlemen sat on lounge chairs and created most of the smoke.

We clubbed till about 3 a.m. and woke up at 8 a.m. the next day; not anyone's intention, certainly not mine. By Auntie's standards, getting up at 8 a.m. meant sleeping in! Her practice is to wake up first and sleep last during every experience I've ever had with her. She generously insisted that I spend the night at her place each time 9 p.m. passed with me there. I consider the repeated experience I have had to be enough data on which to draw my conclusions about her routine.

I used to be a college student whose earliest class was at 9 a.m., which was not a luxury available to many. Then, I never went to bed earlier than 1 a.m. If I didn't have to get up earlier than 10 a.m., I did not. But that changed, and I have since had to get up at 4:30 a.m. for work. Even then, I was not at my best that morning, and Auntie was ready to leave long before we left. My still dripping hair was wrapped in a towel when Matanda and I stepped into an elevator already occupied by a well-dressed, middle-aged gentleman with whom Matanda put her conversational French to practice speaking with him. While they did, I kept my mouth shut. My French proficiency wasn't past what was required at a ballet class for young children.

The gentleman recognised us from the club, having been one of those who had been at the lounge seats. We had a nice laugh about that. When we stepped off the elevator and separated on friendly enough terms, Auntie followed the gentleman. We assumed it was a mutual acquaintance of hers.

She returned after he had gone into the hotel's restaurant for breakfast, telling us we had just met royalty. Would we like to introduce ourselves?

Mortified, we went to the bathroom, where I brushed my hair. But my hair was like a sponge, which soon made the back of my shirt a lost cause. Matanda, in the meantime, applied makeup and stepped into the restaurant, where His Majesty invited us to lunch at his palace. We honoured the invitation. The lunch was delicious. His Majesty had more than one wife, which isn't relevant, but it's one of the things I remember and needed no photograph to prod my memory. The room was gorgeous, and he had something of a museum outside dedicated to his kingdom's history and culture. We took some time exploring it, but since we did not want to be late or outwear our welcome, we took our leave. Besides, a cultural celebration was starting, which may have been rude to stay for. Also, we were told that the celebrations got rather rowdy.

\*\*\*

At this point, the hustle and bustle of the trip's conclusion is blurred. However, I remember that the morning we left Ndop for the last time, I made a video tour of the house on my phone. I regret that Darryl, who followed the car on his bike until that was no longer possible, was not in the video. As to the house in Yaoundé, we left it in a hurry to avoid traffic, owing to the travel arrangement of the president of Cameroon. Because of the somewhat hurried departure, I didn't video the last look of the home.

The irresistible colour and taste of the bananas made us buy a good deal. Matanda and I certainly took more potassium than we needed to finish the tasty bananas we could not afford to waste as we considered them superior specimens of what we had in the US. Pineapples were in season, but we couldn't get them anywhere we went because they had been sold out. We did have mangoes, however.

The fruity luxury contrasted with my laundry supply, which was running on fumes by the time we were at the airport. However, since we were not meeting anyone for the first time that day, I had been reduced from tailored shirts and dress pants to a Snoopy T-shirt and a pair of jeans and trousers. So simply attired and with my companions, I left Cameroon when the sun was going down that early August.

*＊＊*

I'm afraid I was ill at the airport due to the stress of travelling. My mood easily affects my health. I got upgraded to first class, which, in retrospect, means I should have perhaps swapped the offer with another member of my party. I should have done so, especially because I was the one white person in the said party and, unfortunately, probably the relevant reason for the privilege I got. That said, I'm afraid it did not occur to me at the time, and as I had never, I am unlikely to fly first class by paying for it. That consciousness perhaps remotely informed some design in me to milk the opportunity.

Of course, everyone knows that flying first class is a prestige symbol and way too expensive, which is why those there receive amenities that are not available to people in economy class – such as so much food. Besides, I was offered a complimentary drinks menu that included a "Champagne of the Month." I had never drunk champagne before; I only knew this one sounded special. Like my botched resolution to stay awake on the flight east, I also thought that I should try to sleep on the flight west.

Then bread, fruit, and chocolates were all complimentary and not even part of the complimentary three-course meal. I remember taking a fruit salad appetiser, lamb, and something raspberry. They kept plying the guests with booze, bread, chocolate, and fruit between courses. To put it mildly, I was on my way to a food coma, although I still managed to embarrass the host staff by being amazed every time they showed up. The thought of smuggling some of the food back to third class entered my mind, and I indulged in fantasies of more overt food redistribution.

Back to my sleep balance, the seats could lean back, and you could stretch your leg out without hitting the seat in front of you. Even the pillows were less flat, the armrests cushioned, and there was a blanket. Everything was in order, and I slept, only waking up shortly before we landed in NYC.

The gritty part of travelling internationally involved filling out forms inquiring if you had "Anything to Declare." The lines for this were long but soon split, depending on citizenship. By and by, it was over. Uncle came to pick us up from the airport and drove us back to Delaware. Although I had the foggy idea to unpack my bag and leave for our house, it soon became apparent and, quickly too, that I was not fit to drive - not because of the alcohol, but because we were bone exhausted. We fell asleep and woke up at a late hour the next day. Only then did we get to unpack the bags for me to make my exit back to the house I was a sub-letter in. A back view styles the entire experience somewhat as surreal.

\* \* \*

Back home in the United States, it took some time to settle, and after resting, I called my parents, with whom I hadn't spoken since the trip started. That had something to do with the economy of calls. Although I had set up a phone for international calls, the prices made me save those for emergencies. No emergency occurred, and that meant a one-month incommunicado with my parents.

The call to my parents resulted in my meeting Dad at a nearby Chick-fil-A. Even though I do not endorse the restaurant, I craved their chicken, and this was offering me the second fast food meal since returning from Cameroon, the first having been earlier in the week. Familiarity and practice are ways of inducing attachment. I must admit that I missed American food, and it would take less time to start missing Cameroonian food.

When at the Chick-fil-A, my dad asked me about the trip, and different impulses welled up in me. In the first place, I knew the trip was important. Auntie had impressed upon us how rare an opportunity it was, and indeed, so it was. She had elaborated on how insidious and dominant the narratives surrounding the continent usually were.

There were economic as well as racial factors. My mom was unemployed, and my father was middle-class, which meant a lower-middle-class lifestyle. For my father and I, our circumstances result in a certain cynicism towards things that are too good to be true. In a sense, this was quite attested to by our trip. For, hadn't Auntie told us that we were seeing parts of the country that most of its citizens hadn't? Hadn't we met the Prime Minister? For security reasons, we could not roam the streets ourselves.

So, I told my dad the truth as I saw it, which I knew he could believe. However, I had a hard time conveying the highlights of the trips without pictures, which had not yet been distributed at the time. It was, therefore, easier to convey the frustrations of travelling because those were feelings, and I had been frustrated, particularly because, at the risk of being crude, I had been bleeding for three solid weeks. I'm still unsure whether the issue was strictly gynaecological or if medication contributed. In response to my probably incoherent rambling, Dad asked me what he considered the two most important questions.

Am I glad that I went?

Yes.

Would I go again?

I thought about that. There were many countries on earth and only so much time to travel. Probably not, I decided and shoved the rest of the chicken strip in my mouth. But just three years later, I proved myself wrong.

\*\*\*

The first trip had been instigated somewhat circumstantially when, in March 2016, I was walking with Matanda back from Main Street to the library parking lot. Her mother was waiting to pick her up, and when we got there, Mrs Mondoa told us that the trip to Cameroon was happening this summer. She was taking her daughter home, was the message as far as I was concerned, and congratulations were in order. Then she added, "There's more. You're invited."

My reaction was instant and rather visceral. I must have said something like, "Are you kidding me?" The discussion rolled over to the idea of getting permission from my parents. I joked that I had already made up my mind and thanked her. But reality set in immediately the buzz wore off.

First, I was under no financial liberty to travel abroad. For God's sake, I was a graduate student, so I would need not only permission but a loan as well. Necessarily, I brought up the idea. My mom was thrilled—a brilliant woman who has not been on the best side of luck. My going was vicarious wish fulfilment, as far as she was concerned.

Mother's wish was not all there was. I had to come to terms with my sister, who had the strongest adverse reaction. I want to attribute her reaction to her germophobia and the big-sister syndrome of considering me an eternal baby and, therefore, ill-prepared for life's sometimes tough challenges. From her perspective, I was sure to screw up and catch a disease, she indicated. Thankfully, I didn't need to convince her about anything. It was my dad I needed to listen to, and he had valid reservations, essentially due to security concerns, which were understandable from his view as a retired military personnel. Undoubtedly, there were such nasty things on the web about the Boko Haram group.

After all, Dad has never stopped giving what he believed was good for me or my sister. He worked full-time and evening shifts to put my sister and me through college. He had already indulged my wanderlust once before, back in my college days. I had quietly convinced myself I would never get another opportunity to travel outside the country.

When Dad capitulated on my travel request, he immediately announced that I would not expect anything for my birthday or Christmas. Yet, that was just a way of speaking like a lying liar who lies. He is that kind of man who will loudly proclaim that no, we are not adopting that cat, how, as a matter of fact, he ought to shoot it. Yet, inexplicably, he would become that same cat's favourite person, take it to the vet for its shots and have it ensconced in our house and sleeping in his bed.

Christina and I had met for the first time some five months back, in December 2015, having been invited to Matanda's brother's wedding. I still wonder whether she was born with this disposition or developed it; she is both emotionally open and perceptive, and she is one of the few extremely outgoing people I have met who has not entirely overwhelmed me. Because we both knew Matanda, our transition period into friendship was swifter than would be considered normal. We saw *Star Wars: The Force Awakens* in theatres; we got our hair done. We apparently won Auntie over. I found that out later. For the moment, I was seeing Christina for the second time, and it was as we prepared for the trip to Cameroon.

I had already come a long way with Matanda, although I need some clarification about the first time we met. It was probably at a Banned Books table on the South Green at the University of Delaware, and we talked about the censorship of manga (a comic with an artistic style said to originate from Japan). I don't think we exchanged numbers then. Still, we repeatedly met at literacy events and flickered in and out of memory until Spring 2015, when we ended up in the same Contemporary American Theatre class. That is when we swapped numbers with each other and with a classmate named Yvonne, who had fascinating points about the portrayal of femininity in children's animation. I haven't talked to Yvonne in years; however, which indicates how even lovely people get forgotten and how we miss a lot of second chances.

It makes sense that we undertook this trip despite the alternatives of countries in the world and the inimical factors like reservations about the Yellow Fever vaccine and Boko Haram, whether reasonable or not. Christina and I came on this trip for Matanda, our mutual friend. She is the reason we took the trip and did another (2019), and we are prepared for more ad infinitum.

**Sarah Emily Craster** earns a pay cheque teaching because, as she says, 'the devil's in the details and the universe is wonderfully absurd.' A storyteller by compulsion, she exorcises this with her friends, hoping to get to a broader audience when she will pen them down. Her relaxation coping strategy against anxiety is daydreaming while listening to music or playing on the keyboard.

TL: Celebrating at St Elizabeth Ann Seton the day before our trip
TR: Passports out at JFK, and preparing for the first segment of our journey.
BR: Layover at Brussels with a supportive message from MasterCard
BL: Christina and Sarah meet Prime Minister Philemon Yang for the first time.

Sarah, Matanda, Auntie, and Christina join Louis and Melanie for an event

Prime Minister Philemon Yang and Matanda

At The National Museum, Sarah, Matanda, and Christina visit Cameroonian history

Our group waits for Catholic Mass in Yaounde

At CRTV, au coeur de la nation, Matanda, Sarah, and Christina pose as though they have their own show

A quick stop between Bafoussam and Bamenda to behold one of Cameroon's most beautiful waterfalls

After arrival at Bamunka, Darryl and Leo greet Matanda and Sarah

Gathering the rainwater was a bucket of laughs for Matanda, Christina, and Sarah

Sarah, Matanda, and Christina enjoy an afternoon with His Royal Highness, the Fon of the Bamunka kingdom

Christina relishes the smell of fresh tea leaves at Ndawara Highland Tea plantation

A curious examination of tea leaves under the Cameroonian sun

The group climbs up Mount Oku to behold its majesty, Lake Oku

Auntie Rachel opens her arms to receive Lake Oku's welcome to all

Lake Oku in its picturesque glory

Christina and Matanda ask Christian Cardinal Tumi questions, and Sarah is content to listen

Dinner time at Cardinal Tumi's home with Chef David

An afternoon spent sharing music with Uncle Caven and his wife

Matanda standing at St Joseph's College Sasse, Alma Mater of her father, Dr. Emil Mondoa

Sarah, Christina, and Matanda visiting Uncle Willie on the way back to Yaounde

Everyone got dressed up for Matanda's birthday with a visit His Excellency's office

His Excellency receiving Matanda in his office makes for a truly happy birthday

CHAPTER FOUR

**Auntie**

DAD'S WISH FULFILLED

Freedom of choice is something we often underestimate. There is a world of difference between being in one locality for even fifty years, conscious of your liberty to stroll out of it, and being in one place for even an hour punitively or without the liberty of choice to move out. Without the liberty to walk out, even a leisurely walk or visit feels like a prison, a hemmed-in restrictive experience that saps the will of proactive ventures. A little handicap, whether physical or conceptual, can mean significant limitation, especially if the subject refuses to come to terms with it. That is just such a limitation I had when negligence caused me to delay the renewal of my passport. A total lack of response worsened the situation, for I just threw in the towel as it were and dreamily went about life without a thought of the future and the impact of the present on it. But underneath this lacklustre demeanour, there was love for my father, an ailing old man whose looks I could only conjecture fifteen years after our last encounter in 2008 when he last visited the USA.

When, on December 31st, 2015, a friend and I flew from Newark International Airport through Brussels, something clicked. I had not been to Cameroon for 15 years. That trip stirred soul-searching. I was stuck in the United States, willy-nilly, because I hadn't renewed my passport, and the situation had rolled on unendingly, year in and year out. Laziness and a lack of resolve kept me, I would say, somewhat disinterested in correcting the entrapping ditch I was in. I was unsure what to do, or should I say that I didn't care enough to dig up what to do about it until it occurred to me one day.

I was talking to a friend in Canada and just flung it in that my passport could be renewed and that I could visit Cameroon. I just flung it out, but in the meantime, I had a lot of fear in my heart because I did not know if going to Cameroon was the right thing to do at that time. Not having been there for over fifteen years meant that the country was becoming blurry in my imagination. When I was there in 2000, the stay had been relatively brief, and the flurry of quick encounters did not register lasting interest. But in Cameroon were my roots, and rootlessness, like faithlessness, craves re-rooting. A whiff of Augustine's oft-quoted idea of our need for God and our restlessness, until we rest in him, was perhaps a woolly background to this instability of mine.

Love across seas, too, came in. News about my ailing father puffed in with scents of longing. For ten-odd years, it had been his duty to visit me often. Now, he hadn't or wasn't able to. I took a leap of faith. The lack of a passport was still louring, but the decision to visit my ailing father was strong enough. You could call it a meta-psychic resolve, and it worked, and I arrived in Cameroon on New Year's Day 2016.

Right after landing at the Yaoundé airport, I realised that much had been altered. So much had changed, which frightened and cheered me up as I braced myself to reach my old dad. It turned out that the old homeliness of family bonding had stayed on despite the physical changes I had been half scared by. It was a warm couple of days' visit with the family in Yaoundé before I shot up north to my parents, my father having phoned me when I touched ground at the airport. He was looking forward to seeing me, he said. But I had a stronger desire to meet my darling father.

I should say that travelling from Yaoundé to Bamenda was the longest journey; at least, it was such in my mind. For one thing, the public trans-city vehicles were uncomfortable despite the many hours one had to be on the road. Worse, the road for some 100 kilometres was a gullied earth road, the least comfortable thing to imagine riding on.

The home warmth that began in Yaoundé had other concrete advantages and self-sacrificing appendages. In this category should be joined the offer of a friend of mine. An SUV with a driver to take me wherever I wished was one big offer that silenced the dread of the northwest trip home. It was a godsend of pure, non-reciprocal kindness. So, ensconced in the SUV comfort, I answered my father, who called every hour of the journey, a measure of his affectionate concern. The leisure to stop when I cared to do so, and the cushioned protection from the harsh bumps of the gullied earth road made the journey a sheer delight. The delight was lit up by the expected and glowing love I was moving up to at home.

The chauffeur helped to pack out my luggage. As he drove off, I saw that my father had aged quite a bit from the last time I had seen him. It didn't matter that he maintained his usual manner of standing up to greet; he was worn out, so to speak. It was easy to judge why: illness saps and imposes fast ageing characteristics. I didn't nurse any feelings of guilt that I could have helped stem the process. Life was a cycle, and delaying the hand of the clock could only be apparent when it inexorably went its destined route.

My mother, for her part, had her pristine cool as she emerged from the room. You could see that her heart beamed with profoundly authentic joy. I luxuriated for fourteen days in that joy and the heat of my father's paternal care. It was an invigorating experience, one which I dared compare with what near-death or mystical experiencers detail. Of course, those experiences are all about having unconditional love encounters with the oversoul, God, or just other empathetic human beings.

Sweet as the times were, it had only a season. The time soon came for me to return. Ritual consolidates wishes and desires. My father gave me his blessings, ritualised, I should say, for it was emphatic and couched in measured phrases that ended with the caveat, an admonishing tag, that I should come along with my daughter the next time. It wasn't a prescriptive declaration; more, it was suggestive, and the phrase "if possible" removed all compulsion from the request. My daughter had never been to Cameroon. I got the hints with all their force and not only resolved but made a verbal promise to bring her, adding, as all human decisions must be guarded, the phrase "if possible." I would return in June or July with her, I told him, thus pinning my resolve on a timeline.

Resolved, I made sure it happened, hurdles notwithstanding. So, on July 20, 2016, my daughter, her two friends, and one of my friends and I rode on Brussels Airlines to Cameroon, fulfilling my father's wish for me to bring home his granddaughter. The alacrity or panache in fulfilling this wish was in my bringing his granddaughter and two of her friends.

One of these friends of my daughter was travelling out of the United States for the first time. This made me doubly concerned about how the journey impacted them. My daughter and one of her friends would be easy to accommodate, but I wasn't sure of the other. For one thing, she was allergic to many food items. Whatever the case, preparing well for the journey was part of the solution. Thus, it became a high point of the entire venture.

Christina was the de facto leader of the group. She composed a packing list. A commonality not particularly previewed was that all three young girls were singers. They came up with songs, outfits, makeup, and a great deal of niceties for the entertainment of those they expected to meet in Cameroon. In hindsight, they were packaging both joy and gratitude in those niceties, songs and performances they intended to offer.

We had to be meticulous about weights. Each one was to have two pieces of luggage, each weighed to ensure they didn't exceed airline standards. Each item in the suitcase announced the advancing days towards the journey and raised the excitement levels. Neighbours and other community members learned that Christina, Matanda, and Sarah were about to travel to Cameroon, so many thousand miles away. It was no secret but perhaps did not need to be popularised unnecessarily. It is hard to keep excitement secret, which is why most of their community got the exciting news.

As a Christian and Catholic by upbringing, I felt it necessary to usher in the divine. And so, on Tuesday, July 19th, we had Mass with journey mercies as intentions at our home parish church, Saint Elizabeth Ann Seton. The parishioners were very supportive, each expressing their happiness in various ways, but most were curious to know some details about the journey.

A farewell dinner at my home was more restricted; attendees included Auntie Helene, Dr Mondoa, and Rachel. Rachel was accompanying us to Cameroon, being a family friend and member of the Seton Parish. The dinner time was quality time too for information and instructions, particularly to the neophyte girls, on what to expect while going to Cameroon. Everyone was to ensure they had their visas and cross-check the validity of their vaccines. In this respect, Christina's visa was delayed, and she nearly did not travel with us. Thanks to friendly connections with Cameroon's ambassador to Canada, matters were sorted out before it was too late. We were thus set, boxes all packed, weighed, and arranged in the living room. You could say we were athletes waiting for the sprint whistle to go.

At the risk of making this sound like a laundry list or juxtaposed catalogue of activities, on July 20th, we boarded a Delaware Express van to John F. Kennedy Airport. Matanda's dad, Dr Mondoa, transported some of our bags in his van. Upon arrival, we checked in, had dinner and got ready for the first flying lap of the journey. We were seated in the plane by 6:15 p.m. and soon airborne to arrive at Brussels the next morning, July 21st. That is where we had breakfast, the girls rushing for the popular Belgian waffles.

Nothing serious happened before we took another flight from Belgium to Yaoundé via Douala. When we were about to land in Douala, the girls were curious to watch the topography through the window, realising that we were indeed hovering over Cameroon's soil. We spent one hour in the airport before transiting to and landing at the Yaoundé Nsimalen Airport. It was already dark, about 8:00 p.m.

The landing in itself was uneventful, but the significance was immeasurable. It marked, arguably, the happiest day of my life, the day I brought my daughter and her friends home to Cameroon. It was a first for all three girls, and I secretly wondered what their sentiments and reactions to the novelties would be like.

I ensured our smooth movement by prearranging with my nephew, Louis, to receive and take us to an apartment in the Bastos neighbourhood in Yaoundé. Louis had thoughtfully come with two vehicles, a friend of his driving one and he, the other, into which we split and rode. In the excitement of seeing his cousin and her friends, Louis plunged the car into a deep pothole, wedging it stolidly in, deflating one of the tyres in the event.

Our vehicle reached our destination before realising that Louis' car was long in coming. A phone call located them and their straits. The girls and the luggage were moved to the next car while the halted car was attended to.

Finally home, we were received by our friends and Louis's wife, Melanie. Then came dinner, the first Cameroonian food the girls ate in Cameroon. Although it was night, I called to inform Matanda's godfather of our safe arrival, and he immediately invited us to his office the very next day. Worn out, we showered and went to bed, preparing for the next day, a long day.

I got the others up early to do their morning cleaning before a good Cameroonian breakfast of crepes, eggs, avocado, puff-puff, *Ovaltine*, coffee, and tea that visibly enchanted Matanda and her friends. Before long, we were dressed up, and Louis Bukong, Matanda's cousin who had ferried us from the airport, took us out. First, we went to a ceremony, an installation or school event where we were treated to some interesting home traditional music. The beautiful dress of the attendees was also piquing. I knew quite a few of those we met there and exchanged pleasantries with them before we left the occasion midway to respond to Matanda's godfather's invitation.

Because our names had already been given at the gate, our check-in to see him was speedy. Ever gracious, the statesman received us right at the door, hugging the children, although, as a rule, he did not hug visitors. Technically, he was not breaking any rule, for Matanda, being his god-daughter, was, in principle, family. Besides, he had kept inviting Matanda to come to Cameroon until this time when the force of my dad's invitation made it impossible to resist.

We hardly had more than 40 minutes to visit with him, as he was a busy statesman and head of government with tight schedules to cover. It was enough time for the girls to take turns asking him questions and receiving answers. He briefed them about Cameroon's past, and they discussed some academic and cultural differences and music.

From the Prime Minister's office, we touched base for lunch, after which we went to the Cameroon National Museum to expose Cameroon's past, arts and crafts to the girls. The displayed paintings and artefacts, enhanced by the guide's commentary, were certainly great enlightenment to them. Practice and knowledgeability equipped the guide with apt answers to their numerous questions about the displayed items. The girls were treated to the fascinating fabrics that represented the different regions they were culled from. Coincidentally, the day corresponded with the celebration of the life and achievements of Cameroon's icon, Anne Marie Nzie. A film festival was also taking place on the museum's grounds. It was late afternoon when we left the museum to go home and prepare for church service the next day, which was Sunday.

We took a taxi to the Catholic Church, and Louis and Melanie joined us later in the service. The offertory procession caught the attention of the girls, and church over, greetings followed. We also took pictures with some members of the church outside before we returned home to food and relaxation. A handful of my friends and classmates visited, and we had fun, the girls singing for entertainment.

I had been considering places that would interest the girls for some time, and the Cameroon Radio and Television (CRTV) was an attraction. So, we went there the very next day and were gracefully received by Mr Robert Ekukole, a schoolmate of Dr Mondoa's. We could read his pleasure in receiving us as he welcomed us to his office and showed us around the broadcasting complex. The interest points included the girls getting into the production room to play role-playing.

I also pleasantly met my classmate; it was our mutual joy that I was visiting the broadcasting house. Then the girls gave their gift, a performance of one of their songs, before we took a taxi home. Home would not be much rest, however, for we had to get set for the trip to Bamunka, Ndop, way up some 350 miles north-westerly from Yaoundé. Early the next morning, we packed our bags in a vehicle provided to us by a friend. It was the measure of our purposefulness that by 7:00 a.m., we were all dressed up and on our way to Bamenda.

The driver, Mr Gilbert, was not only a lovely person who interacted in an informed way with us as if we had known him for a long time; he was also skilful and experienced at driving and knew the roads well. Driving from Yaoundé to our destination meant shifting from different geographical peculiarities to others. First, there was the immediate forest density. This gradually gave way to less dense forests and then to the savanna. The marker that we were out of the centre region seemed to have been the large Sanaga River, about a mile wide. So far, up to the roadside town of Makenene, the topography generally had no hills worth noting.

We stopped at Makenene, which was technically a stopping point and somewhat in the middle of the journey. It was a roadside boomtown where we could use the bathroom. The hygienic conditions of such wayside conveniences were going to be questionable, but the girls decided to take a chance. It was an experience of what a public and dirty bathroom could look like. True, it had been somewhat cleaned but clearly had known better days. In fact, it was when the lady who ran the place saw the girls, she pulled a bucket and cleaned the toilets.

The floor was eroded and reeked of urine fumes. It was a taste of roadside life where hygiene was not a priority. You answered nature's call without fuss, which clearly emphasised our basic humanity devoid of the flourishes of finesse. The state of the bathroom did not alter our enjoyment of the hot food and drinks we bought from the road-aligned stalls. Our journey was jolly, and life was good; the people were friendly, and we went our merry way.

We continued to the outskirts of the city of Bafoussam at the Mifi waterfall, a sight to see. We went down to the scenic waterfall and took pictures, the girls swishing postures and making recordings of the alluring spectacle. It was one of those brief moments that make the plodding stretches of life less inimical. It was not a totally isolated setting to raise security issues, for some locals were around.

Enlivened thus by nature at its soothing stability, we continued to Bamenda, another but not-so-memorable stop occurring somewhere along the line. In Bamenda, we stopped briefly and then continued to Ndop as evening was coming on. The girls couldn't miss the ravaging topography of Sabga, however. The hill ranges enacted a complex symmetry of slants, ledges, gigantic but stark rocks and valleys in waves that seemed to have no end and yet formed a synchronised hemispheric cast of pristine theatre for what must have been a stage for enactments only gods could have performed. The girls got out and were lost in its splendour. I guess the geologist could tell them of the turbulence of volcanoes aeons gone by that brought this wonder of nature into being. A few unimpressive trees punctuated the predominant savanna swards on the undulations.

From Bamenda, Sabga descended about two miles to the Ndop plain. At the foot of the hill was the first village of the plain, Bamessing, famous for pottery and snake charming. Bamessing ran on for a few miles, and then Bamunka proper after an isthmus of another village, Bamali, reared a less than one-mile projection onto the way between Bamessing and Bamunka.

Before long, we were at my father's, Matanda's grandfather's compound. He stood out to welcome us, elated that his eyes, at last, were laid on his granddaughter Matanda at home. Such sentiments are, of course, lost to the absence of words except by links with history or other emotional high points in record. In my mind, this was the kind of encounter Simeon in the Bible must have had upon seeing the baby Jesus at the presentation in the temple that prompted his famous *nunc dimittis*. It might be presumptuous on my part to pair the messianic with this puny local experience, but for the experiencer, it is total emotion that sweeps them off and there is no comparison too big to measure totality with.

Auntie Rachel Joko cooked some food with my mother, and my aunt, Theresa, was there, as well as Aunt Prudencia. Matanda met her cousins Darryl and Leo when they arrived at the house. The home was in a festive mood of warm welcomes with endless chatting. Eventually, beds beckoned, and rest was necessary. Sarah and Matanda took up my mom's room; my mom and I moved to a guest room, and Christina had a room to herself. The festive atmosphere continued throughout the next day, and in the evening, the three girls sang to my dad during his dinner time. My brother-in-law, who came visiting that evening accompanied by his son, Laka, sat in the living room and enjoyed the singing. Joy pervaded everything as lively chatting and stories from my dad graced the hours. So, the day passed and another night. The following day, we were invited to the palace.

Casual as the invitation looked, it turned out to be of utmost significance. As culture dictated, we didn't go to the palace empty-handed but took along some alcoholic drinks as a present to His Majesty. When we arrived, the king was out, and we took the opportunity of his absence to visit the queens, one of whom showed us around. She was well-informed, and her explanations were boosted with hearty friendliness. We were well-edified and were taken to see the palace inside, a complex setting with symbolic items and esoteric, historical, and cultural values.

On the historical plain, we were shown pristine hand machinery that used to be the corn mill. The esoteric component included secret coves within the palace. All we saw were paintings, masks, and old furniture that had come from the line of previous kings. The living room of the palace had antiques, carvings, beads, and other artwork of the locale. These had intricate patterns of significance to the people of the area. There were pictures too of the former king, and there were wild animal skins, including those of the leopard and boa constrictor. On the hallway wall hung a particular traditional talisman that was said to ward off evil spirits from entering the palace.

Time went on, and it was as if we had come for sightseeing at the palace rather than on invitation. As we took pictures at the entrance to the palace with the background of significant trees, we were informed that His Majesty was back and was asking for us at another residence a stone's throw from the palace setting. We drove there and were warmly welcomed and treated to drinks. His Majesty was visibly elated and hugged each of the girls, treating them as family kids, for, by custom, the king didn't hug people.

Moments passed, and the king entertained us with tales for a while. On his invitation, some people came in, and we left for Matanda's aunt's house. Our next stop was at Karl Njoko, my brother-in-law's beautiful residence. Apart from the appealing architectural design, the house's interior had uniquely captivating locally made carvings. We had dinner at the Njokos, where Mrs. Rachael Njoko treated us to some exceptional Cameroonian cuisine. She is an excellent cook and I could tell she had learnt well from our mother, Mrs. Anthonia Kweh, a super-skilled and exquisitely gifted cook. Tired as we were, there was a major trip before us the following day. We spent the night with it in mind - the trip to Lake Oku.

Breakfast and goodbyes set us en route to Lake Oku from where we intended to return that same day. We drove to Babungo, which lay on the highway to Kumbo in the Bui Division. Oku was under Bui, but a quicker road forked from the highway and through Babungo to the lake. It is, however, a virtually unrelieved and often quite steep ascent from there to Mount Oku. So steep was the incline that it was sometimes scary as the vehicle seemed to be on the verge of tipping over every so often. Thanks to his familiarity with the road (hailing from Oku) and driving expertise, Mr Gilbert navigated the dangers with composure.

We eventually reached the peak on top of the mountain and engaged the second leg of the journey to Lake Oku, a crater lake up the 2,227-metre-high Mount Oku and hemmed in by forests. It is an eerie setting that lends itself to myths and legends among the indigenous people. No life seems to survive in the

600-acre surface and 53-metre-deep lake except the strange and unique clawed frog. We left the car and walked down the steps to the lake.

Attractive as Lake Oku was, our prime destination was the Ndawara Tea Estate. The attractions there (the expanse of the setup, the tea processing, and the zoo) made us spend more time there than we had expected. We had parked by the owner's home, a beautiful British castle-style structure. It certainly had many rooms, but you could say that the structure stood in the middle of nowhere, for the only other structures were the tea processing factory and tiny houses in the distance, home to the many factory workers. The workers we met were adequately informed of the processes involved in the tea production. The stopover was crowned by a sit down during which marketing fabric of the estate were given to us along with some packets of tea.

When we had the easy walk to the lake then, we were already down on time. Nonetheless, we had to give each place its due. The lake, being our destination, was not something to hurry over. The steps down the lake were solid and clear. We found the water in the quiet of that afternoon so clean that for peering, it was easy to see right down to the bottom of the lake. True, mirror images of the surrounding trees did play on the edges. The experience left one with depth and a feeling of the unfathomable and mysterious. So, we took our sobering thoughts to the local market, where indigenes sold various items. It would be rather hurried and self-defeating to rush back in the dark, the rugged and steep incline of the road we had had on our way to the place to boot. Common sense dictated that we spend the night in a hotel near the lake. July was the heart of the rainy season, not a season for tourists, so we were the lone occupants in the 100-room hotel.

At those heights, and with the scanty population, the coldness of the setup was especially heightened at night after we made our pick of rooms. The dinner served included the fried intestines of the chicken, which took the girls aback, but a little explanation settled them. Dinner over and the strain of the trip taking its toll, we were about to sleep when it started raining. The sheer weight of the raindrops was a curiosity to the girls. They came out of their rooms and used torchlights to watch what was, for them, a wonder.

As it turned out, passing the night was a good idea because, in the morning, we were able to take a second look at the lake. The atmosphere indeed modified the morning look of this mysterious outlay of water. Be that as it may, we were taking samples of it in plastic bottles as proof of our encounter with this mountain wonder.

Back home to Bamunka, we narrated our previous day's experiences. My father was not feeling well this evening. I cannot say that the *nunc dimittis* hint took hold of me to inspire any foreboding. He took some medication, and we spent two more days with him before getting ready to return to Yaoundé. There was an element of urgency in this back trip to Yaoundé because Christina had to return to the States. My father looked fine when we left, and we stopped in Bamenda to see Mr Willie Kimbeng, who received us warmly and offered us refreshments of peanuts and African plum. During the hour we spent here, the girls had the opportunity to deliver a song for his pleasure.

It was time to be gone. The rugged road from Bamenda to Bafoussam struck us anew as uncomfortable, but, by and by, it was over, and we reached Yaoundé, on the way resting a while in Bafoussam before continuing to Makenene where we had another break. There, the girls had a fresh look at the panoply of local foodstuffs - plantains, African plums, shish kebabs, cookies, and various snacks. Again, the girls used the smelly roadside bathroom, and we continued our journey blissfully.

We finally reached the house in Yaoundé, acknowledging Mr Gilbert's driving expertise. However, we were missing out on one major blessing, without which we would have had many police checkpoint breaks and delays—the friend's car we were using. Not even one checkpoint stopped our car, a thing the girls were likely oblivious to.

The following day, we had a call on Matanda's godfather, and again, he had time to converse with the girls. Then we decided to see how he got home, his car having no number on the silver plates. The glasses on the windows were tinted so you couldn't see its occupant. What was most remarkable was the snap accuracy of the happenings, much like lightning as the motorcade was led by two vehicles in front of his and followed by one behind.

After the spectacle of his departure was over, we went to the Hilton Hotel, where we had a pre-planned dinner date to celebrate Matanda's birthday before departing for Douala the next day. We left early for Douala.

Without incident, we arrived in Douala and visited a friend of mine for about an hour before going to Christian Cardinal Tumi's residence, which was like home to us. The cardinal was resting when we arrived, but our noisy arrival woke him up, and he came to meet us. Aunt Rachel Kanla met us there a little later for dinner, chatter, and a lot of fun. We were with the Cardinal all of the next day but left for Buea the day after. We had to spend two days in Buea, where our resting place was the Buea Mountain Hotel. While Christina slept, we visited the alma mater of Matanda's dad - St. Joseph's College, Sasse. We also visited the sister school, Bishop Rogan's College, meeting the bishop of Buea, His Lordship Emmanuel Bushu, a most gracious and receptive man of God. Sarah sang him a song he enjoyed before we returned to the hotel for dinner and sleep. We prepared to go to Limbe early the next day after breakfast at a local restaurant, but it rained heavily. So, we visited the Mondoa home and observed the rooms. Matanda was keen to see her father's abode when he was in his teens.

Instead of going to Limbe as initially scheduled, we went to Kumba, where we visited the retired mayor of the city, Mr Caven Nnoko Mbelle. His beautiful wife, Auntie Agatha, was very welcoming, and we had a really good time with the couple. Although it was raining, the retired mayor offered to show us around parts of Kumba. We followed him in our car and later returned to Buea.

Thereafter, it was a matter of getting to Yaoundé and passing through Douala. Christina needed to be back in the States. We took her to the Nsimalen Airport to board the plane. We only left after her plane had taken off.

The next day, I got a call from my sister informing me that my dad had had an operation. It wasn't pleasant news by any standard. I needed to be there to assess the situation. So, once more, the very next morning, we were on our way to Bamenda. First of all, we shopped in the market for items we thought my father would need. We found him in good spirits, although he had lost much weight. We were encouraged by his looks, and later, we were misinformed that he had been discharged. We found this false and left with Mr Gilbert, for Ndop the next day before returning the day after.

In the meantime, my sister, Mrs. Joko's husband, Mr. Carl Joko, took Sarah and Matanda to visit his farm. This rural farming experience expanded their worldview of fresh cocoa and guava plants and the valley they had to descend. It offered an excellent contrast to the festal atmosphere that characterised preparations for the wedding of Dr Conrad, MD, a cousin to Matanda. It was a swishing and switching of activities as we had to visit my father in the hospital before returning to don the wedding party dresses and attend the cathedral wedding occasion. The celebratory part of the wedding offered the opportunity for the girls to showcase their singing performance amidst the other tributary dances and other shows there. Amidst all this were some well-dressed boys who came dancing but were said to be disguised thieves- another eye-opening situation for the girls and I.

A nightclub was in the hotel basement, and the girls, chaperoned by Mr. Gilbert, went there. Auntie Rachel Kanla and I were too tired for that, so we slept in. Apart from the fun, the girls encountered a handful of people, one of whom turned out to be royalty, whom the girls recognised from the respectful greeting posture I offered him. He was the king of Babungo. We accepted his invitation to visit his palace, where two of his queens provided us with meals. We also visited his museum, which was quite close to the palace and housed unique carvings, some of which were considered sacred. Apparently, there was some event to take place at the palace, which we could decipher from the visitors, and the trial dancing was already on. So, we excused ourselves and returned to Ndop en route to Yaoundé through Bamenda because we had to have a final look at my father, who was still at the hospital. I asked my dad whether I should stay back and care for him, but he was categorical about taking the girls back to the US.

With Dad's blessings, therefore, we headed for Douala. We had a Mass offered for us there, and the Cardinal officiated it himself. A reception followed this, and we spent two more nights at the Cardinal's residence before finally taking off for Yaoundé. Djeuga Palace was our hotel of choice, but we again visited Matanda's godfather in his office. In the evening, Auntie Rachel Kanla met us for dinner and the final preps for the trip back to the US.

Because the president of the Republic of Cameroon was on his way from his village, traffic and security were going to be quite an issue, so we left early for the airport to avoid the hazards of timing that could ensue. As expected, we had some idle wait before boarding the plane to Brussels and connecting to New York, where Dr Mondoa came to pick us up to Delaware.

Such is the catalogue, as I remember, of our trip and the stops in Cameroon. What lives on now is memory, the post-visit memory of Cameroon for me being more than country and culture. It is a sense of life that flows in my very blood. The words of everyone I met moved beneath my skin, extending to pieces of my soul and bringing my Cameroonian journey far beyond 2016.

Each encounter left its impact, sometimes not easy to put in words; often not physicalised but as an undercurrent of influence and impact. Thus, meeting Mr Philemon Yang nudged me on how critical it is to continue learning. In this respect, education reawakens its pristine value as the gateway to new beginnings, opportunities and enriched global outlook.

Meeting His Royal Highness jostled an awakening of the humbleness of great power. In that encounter, some things were emphatically so precious that they were only to be shared with the most trusting of eyes. I guess this awesome fact informs the sacredness of ritual and the sacredness of marriage bonds. It is the wisdom of ceremonial progress markers like certificates and valedictions and the bonding depths of schoolmates and friends.

Visiting the Cardinal with the girls was a high point of all times in the visit. They got to ask him questions of profound importance to them and experienced him in his own setting. It was a unique, once-in-a-lifetime opportunity for them, a conclusion they arrived at after the Cardinal died. The world press and musicians celebrated him, and his funeral was attended by prelates from all over the world, which spoke to the fact that the girls had visited and interacted with a true prince of the Roman Catholic Church. The encounter has undoubtedly been at the back of Matanda's resolve to study theology at Harvard and bonded her more solidly in friendship with her companions with whom she visited the Cardinal.

**Ambrosia Kweh Mondoa** holds hard to the eternal nature and invincibility of wisdom expressed in kindness and freely given, without noise or hyped visibility. Thus, while experience teaches best, she holds silence as golden and a sturdy stalwart of resourcefulness.

# CHAPTER FIVE

## Christina

## ON SISTERHOOD AND STORYTELLING

Long before we left for Cameroon, Aunty asked Matanda, Sarah, and me to sing as a part of the trip. Performances would be our gifts to everyone we visited, particularly as Matanda and I had gained notoriety while singing together in Delaware. For me, it would be an opportunity to do something more significant: turning the three of us into a band of balladeers. We would have our trios, duos, and solo pieces. We would have a crafted persona and coordinating outfits to show each host more than just a song. We would give them something as close as possible to a concert at Carnegie Hall. Our repertoire would extend from classic rock and pop radio to Broadway classics, each host receiving songs they could choose. Any sound they wanted, we could produce, for we were their performers, giving thanks for their open homes.

Each element of our musical preparation required joint exploration of what attributes we wanted to show— how we could do it on a united front. One of the most critical elements of this presentation would be our fashion. Outfits had to be expressive yet poised, given the American reputation of sloppiness.

It was essential that our fashion be ready for every eventuality while staying emblematic of our individual selves.

Aunty approved all outfits for sleekness, and approval by the entire group for a coordinated set was the seal. By the time our attire was put together, we had a name extending beyond styles and into musical personas for our sets: *Retro Glamazon* for me, *Nerd Couture* for Matanda, and *Masculine Chic* for Sarah. Once that preparation for our shows was complete, we needed to ensure our voices sounded as good as we looked. Even in the solo pieces, we worked as a group to ensure that the soloist shone with confidence.

Music kicked off our Cameroon trip long before our feet crossed JFK's threshold. For a church service the night before we left, Matanda, Sarah, and I sang *Seasons of Love* from *Rent*. A song in which love was the resounding answer for measuring and evaluating the course of one's life. It was met with thunderous applause, extending beyond the church's pews to the people we met across the Atlantic.

My mind goes back to Cameroon every time I hear *Seasons of Love* because of how often we shared it with every person we met. His Excellency, His Royal Highness, His Eminence, The Secretary of State, Network Executives, and the Mountain Hotel, where Princess Diana and Prince Charles once stayed. The entirety of the Cameroon airport right before I left Yaounde, preparing myself to depart for performance pursuits in Los Angeles. All of them heard one of our favourite songs and the unified anthem of our hearts as we offered our hosts extensions of the sisterhood. It showcased the love that bound us together for our unified travel and continues uniting us to this day.

*Seasons of Love* was not the only musical number that thrilled others. Before we visited the man we knew as Uncle Caven, Aunty told us how much he loved The Beatles. When we sang to him, we saw how the music rang through his heart. Being a Beatlemaniac, it was inevitable that Beatles songs would be mandatory for our repertoire. However, it was quite a surprise to see Uncle Caven stand and sing with us during *All You Need is Love*. Once he joined our group, every person in our gathering was swept away in song, caught up in the message and the meaning lived by a group of sisters. As we learned later, Uncle Caven was once in a Cameroonian Beatles tribute band. Our song choice was the best because he was the group's John Lennon, and *All You Need is Love* is one of John's signature songs.

I dream of the day I would see Uncle Caven again, remembering his joy at the three of us singing The Beatles. There is so much music for us to share and a myriad of Beatles songs to make us "Come Together."

My passion for music makes it so central, and it took on a second form as we travelled from place to place. Watching your sisters sing is like watching a flower opening to full bloom, showcasing its colours to all who are courageous enough to look. It was the case for Sarah and Matanda as they sang, *Girl, Put Your Records On* by Corrine Bailey Rae.

I never heard it before our trip, but it has become a song that recreates the walls of every place we visited and the Cameroonian air on my skin. Sarah and Matanda had so much fun when singing together that it was impossible for me not to snap or clap along, spreading the spirit to everyone who watched. Alongside the feel and colours of each location, I remember the length of both their smiles and how applause warmed their hearts. Cameroon brought out a new spirit in my sisters' voices. For me, no matter how sad I am on any given day, it is impossible not to smile at the thought of them singing together.

I return to *Seasons of Love*, though, because it feels like the music that best epitomised the love we grew together in our journey. Whenever I talk to anyone about our trip to Cameroon, I always mention *Seasons of Love*. I see the faces of Aunty, Matanda, and Sarah whenever I hear the opening notes, my heart swelling with the abundance of familial love I could hardly dream was possible. The love runs so deep that when challenged by anyone, it rises higher in our pulse to stand together.

When catty people ask Matanda and Sarah, "how do you feel singing up there with a professional?" After our performances, we respond that all of us feel amazing. Just like the friendships that defined the Beatles, our performances are defined by family. On any stage we choose, we are family first, and that depth of love shines through our music. Cameroon united my sisterhood in strength and song in a resilient, unbreakable bond. In appearance, support, and singing side-by-side, Matanda, Sarah, and I are united and we will stay that way for as long as we are cognizant and alive.

*\*\*\**

When people hear the word "disabled," the last thing they are likely to picture is a young woman adventuring through Cameroon with her two best friends. Even some of the bolder able-bodied people I know shudder at the thought of traveling to Africa. They build a barrier around themselves far worse than disability, for it keeps them from experiencing the beauty of African cultures and landscapes. Stereotypes are far more restrictive than any difference in body, and I left those far behind for adventure on the horizon. With my two sisters, Matanda and Sarah, and Aunty and Aunty Rachel as watchful second mothers, the world was ours. All barriers were broken.

Together, we did things most people across abilities would find hard to fathom. We toured a tea plantation, starting with fresh leaves on a conveyor belt and ending with packed boxes. We all climbed to the top of a volcano and peeped into its aquatic heart, but I was the only one to do it in high-heeled shoes. Aunty's introductions allowed us to sing for Cameroon's highest officials, including Prime Minister Yang and Cardinal Tumi. In a moment of silliness, Matanda, Sarah, and I played peekaboo with gibbons in a miniature zoo. However, an adventure that stands out to me was taking a shower, a seemingly small action that gave a new purpose to life with disability and illness.

The occasion was a visit to Matanda's grandparents and Aunty's parents in a small village outside Bamenda. To shower there, it was necessary to collect rainwater in a bucket and heat it to near boiling temperatures. Thankfully, we were visiting Cameroon in the heart of the rainy season. Matanda, Sarah, and I collected rainwater for a small portion of our stay, the three of us laughing through every storm. Aunty heated the water for us, the steam swirling with every step as she brought it through the hall. I could feel the hug of each droplet across my skin, a welcome treat after long walks through villages and valleys.

Most people I know would be intimidated and overcome by fragility at the thought of showering with rainwater from a bucket. I took one look at it and said, "Piece of cake!"

Years of washing my hair in the sink and a plastic cup had prepared me for this moment. As a child with chronic ear infections, the sink was the only thing I could use to wash my hair safely to keep water from touching my ears. One wrong droplet brushing against my ruptured eardrums, and I would be screaming in agony. The pain would be felt all through my head, bursting behind my eyes and burning all down my ears and the walls of my throat. Any agony experienced while healthy would be made a thousand times worse if I got water in my ears while they were infected. I was given custom-made earplugs to help, but they would eventually leak as I grew because my ears changed shape and size. There were times when to combat this problem, I started washing my hair in the shower and finished up in the sink, meticulously avoiding any droplets entering my ears.

I kept up with this technique, even as I had my eardrums repaired. Although healing the ruptures allowed me to get water in them with little to no pain, cleaning my scalp around my ears was still the issue. A tympanoplasty (ear surgery to repair a hole in the eardrum) can cause the outer ear to be hypersensitive to the nature of the procedure. One accidental touch or little brush can send you into a spinning world of agony that tingles even your guts. Returning to my old technique, I used the sink to wash around my scars with a lowered risk of pain. I could not rub it hard enough to rid the area of all the greasiness, but I considered any contact with soap and water as better than having none at all.

Not once did I think my sink-washing routine would be suitable for anything other than preventing pain. Only once I went to Bamenda did I see how it could be used beyond life with disability and illness.

My shower consisted of a bottle of TresSemme, two buckets of warm water, and a small dish to pour it over my head. I knew exactly what to do in this setup because it was identical to the one I used to protect my ears. With great confidence, I hung up the towel, reached for the dish, and poured water over my head. Each scoop of water made me feel that my years of suffering had found a way to serve a greater purpose. Better than a cure, I had a means to travel through new places with greater adaptability, allowing me to find a home away from home.

I laughed joyously as a point of pain transformed into one of pride. Each rub of shampoo and splash of steaming water was a victory through an adventure. Between the amazing salve of the warm water and the unexpected freedom from past routines, I never wanted that shower to end.

After towel-drying my hair and bounded into Matanda and Sarah's room, I could not stop talking about what happened. They shared my excitement, laughed with me, and we gave sisterly bear hugs to each other. Days later, when we left Bamenda to return to our apartment in Yaoundé, Aunty said she was amazed by our adaptability to the novelties and challenges in the village. No smile was big enough to show my satisfaction as I absorbed praise for adaptation. One technique had opened my whole world, and what once seemed like weakness had instead become strength.

The dread of many things—whether it's a disability or a new country—is rooted in fears of the unknown, or worse, something only known through stereotypes. Many seek comfort in these ideas rather than challenging them. Fear becomes its own security blanket, and stereotypes become a one-dimensional world map. Those who live according to both create their own barricades rather than looking to see how they can grow. They overlook how adversity can transform into adaptability and act as a key to other ways of life. The greatest "you can't" is not a different kind of body but a mind that chooses to stay in one place.

Had I not learned this lesson through disability, I may never have been able to embrace life in Cameroon. Days of laughing while gathering rainwater may have been lost to Western stereotypes. Friends and smiles from family gatherings may have stayed hidden in the darkness of fear. The doors to my mind may have stayed closed forever had I not learned the importance of adaptability in childhood showers. People may say you do something "in spite of" disability, but the only "in spite of" I faced on my trip was the fear people in the U.S. have about other countries. Being disabled in Cameroon showed me how much "you can't" comes more from others' fears rather than reality. I can, not just because disability taught me to adapt but also because adaptability allowed me to see all the beauty that's held in Cameroon.

\*\*\*

Christian Cardinal Tumi is the reason I was accepted into a prestigious writers' conference, Middlebury Bread Loaf, in Sicily. Three years after meeting him in 2016, I submitted a section of my novel that was directly influenced by our conversation about sin. Everyone in my travelling crew and some of his staff was surprised that I asked His Eminence so many questions. I thought to myself, "This is a man of great wisdom. I want to learn everything I can from him when we are together." As it turned out, Cardinal Tumi's definitions of sin were the building blocks I used to get through a bout of writer's block about a fight between the protagonists.

When he described sin, Cardinal Tumi made a point of presenting its definition through three questions:

"Was the intent of the action to cause harm?"

"Was there understanding of the harm that could be caused when the action was committed?"

"Is there any intention to do this action again if there is understanding of how it caused harm?"

While these questions remained in my mind for years, they

circulated into my fiction during the Spring of 2018. I found myself at a crossroads when writing my novel because I wrote a plot point that seemed unforgivable. I knew I had to bring them back together because there would be no story if they broke up, but I wasn't sure how to make a solution possible at the time. Desperate to ensure my story could work, I turned to Sarah and Matanda for help.

I told them about my envisioned conflict for the protagonists, Luca and Cassandra. They fight because Cassandra won't listen to a doctor's directions, and the aftermath results in her destroying Luca's shoes. Understandably, Luca is upset and tells her it's all her fault for being sick. Cassandra's interpretation of Luca's words is that he blames her for being chronically ill in the first place. This idea is considered ableist or extremely disrespectful towards disabled individuals. Consequently, Cassandra shuts him out, and he's heartbroken by her unwillingness to speak to him.

Matanda was the first to point out cultural differences within the structure of the two leads. Luca is from Sicily, where ableism is not discussed in the same depth as in America. Cassandra is well versed in ableism as a concept after one of her best friends, Mabel, explains it to her after she survives disability-based abuse. With experience teaching English as a Second Language, Sarah also noted that translating between two languages could cause misunderstandings. Luca could unintentionally say something ableist if he struggled to translate his thoughts from Italian into English. Together, Matanda and Sarah used this information to bring me back to the tenets of sin.

In thinking about them, we reviewed Luca's motivations behind his misstep and what understanding it would take for Cassandra to forgive him.

Was the intent of the action to cause harm?

No.

Luca was upset that Cassandra hadn't listened to the doctor's advisory about nausea prevention. What he intended to do was point out that she ruined his shoes unnecessarily by eating too soon before a balance test. If Cassandra had done as the doctor instructed, she would not have been sick in the first place. All Luca wanted to do was point out how ignoring the doctor made her sick, but she took his words as continued blame for being chronically ill.

Was there an understanding of the harm that could be caused when the action was committed?

No.

Luca's knowledge of ableism was minimal when he lost his temper. It never occurred to him that "it's your fault for being sick" could be interpreted as someone saying, "you brought your chronic illness on yourself." He also had no idea how badly Cassandra had been abused because of her illness. Combined with difficulties in speaking English, it was a disastrous recipe for causing unintended harm. When Cassandra refuses to talk to him, Luca is heartbroken because he doesn't understand why she's shutting him out.

Is there any intention to do this action again if there is understanding of how it caused harm?

No.

Before Luca even understood what he did wrong, he was desperate to apologise. Fabrizio, his younger brother, can help mediate because he's one of Cassandra's best friends and is well-versed in ableism through their friendship. Understanding why both people are hurt, Fabrizio helps Cassandra see how "it's your fault for being sick" does not always mean blame for chronic illness. Mabel supports what Fabrizio tells her and encourages

Cassandra to show Luca compassion.

"Please don't tell me you're still scared of Luca leaving you because you're sick," Fabrizio continued, "He's heartsick because he thinks you're going to leave him."

"What?" Cassandra asked.

"Sì, Luca cried and cried and cried when he couldn't reach you. Luca knows he did something to make you sad, but he doesn't understand what, and when you don't talk to him about why, he's devastated."

"I don't know if I could stay with someone who says such awful things about me when I'm sick, though…"

"Cassandra," Mabel said, "The process of unlearning ableism is lifelong, and not only is Luca further behind, but he's also trying to unlearn ableism in a second language. Combine all of this with someone who is readjusting his Wilson's Disease management in a new country, and he's going to make a lot more mistakes than we ever did."

"Luca may not understand why you're hurt," Fabrizio chimed in, "but he's very remorseful about hurting you."

From the Cardinal's words, I learned how to write an outcome for Cassandra to open her heart to Luca again. The three tenants of sin were crucial in helping Cassandra forgive Luca and see him outside the lens of past traumas. Luca redeemed himself in Cassandra's eyes, and their relationship moved forward, proving that forgiveness is essential to love achieving its full bloom.

At the time, I incorporated Cardinal Tumi's principles into my writing, but it was only to ensure the romance between Luca and Cassandra could continue. What I did not anticipate was that the Cardinal's wisdom would make the disability experience accessible to nondisabled people. The universality of struggles to forgive and define sin allowed participants in Bread Loaf across all abilities to sympathise with both Cassandra and Luca.

All of the participants knew what it meant to be hurt by miscommunication and the difficulty of finding forgiveness. Through this shared experience, they understood how something can appear ableist, what it means to unlearn ableism, and how forgiveness helps us grow within that learning process. I had never considered this until I was actually thanked by other participants for teaching them so much. Truthfully, they needed to thank Cardinal Tumi.

The wisdom embedded by His Eminence fundamentally changed me as a writer and opened up new parts of the world. Cardinal Tumi is the reason I gained enough talent for a writer's conference like Bread Loaf to accept me into their cohort. I am doubtful I would have found the answers for my fiction had I not heard his three questions about sin. There would be no story to share nor opportunity to educate others about disabled life without the universality of his questions. One day in Cameroon has extended into thousands of days of growth in literary and physical worlds. It is all the more reason I await the day I can return with Sarah and Matanda, where we will grow together and share the Cameroonian wisdom that has changed our lives. No doubt about it, I will emerge from every trip to Cameroon a better writer, a better teacher, and a better person.

**Christina Margaret Lisk** is committed to disability advocacy in the non-profit sector and the arts. She has publications in various channels, including The Mighty, Yahoo Finance, and Hearinglikeme.com and a short story in *Nothing Ever Happens in Fox Hollow Anthology*: Vol 2. Her disability love story is a novel in progress, which, in 2019, she presented at Middlebury Bread Loaf in Sicily. Outside of this, Christina epitomises "I'm going to die petting something I shouldn't," referring to dogs and cats which overfill her phone and which she pet sits, no matter where.

## ABOUT THE AUTHORS

**Matanda Mondoa** was born in the United States to two Cameroonian parents. She recently graduated with a Master's degree and Certificate in World Religions from Harvard University. She attended Bryn Mawr College and obtained her Bachelor's degree in English from the University of Delaware. She has such a wide variety of interests that she was nicknamed 'Encyclopedia Matandica'. Whenever she's not going down the research rabbit hole, she livestreams games and commentary on her YouTube and Twitch channels (*DJ MK Off the Air, tandersiah*), studies Japanese, and goes on adventures with her friends and family. *Seasons of Sisterhood* is her first non-academic publication.

**Kanla Rachel Ngeh** is a dedicated professional with a strong foundation in both academia and community engagement. Born and raised in Kumbo, Cameroon, she completed her primary and secondary education in Kumba before earning a Bachelor of Science in Sociology and Anthropology with a minor in General Business from the University of Buea.

Seeking new opportunities, Kanla immigrated to the United States, where she contributed to her community through volunteer work with organizations such as the Bui Family Union and Africana. Her commitment to lifelong learning led her to pursue a Master's of Business Administration with a concentration in Healthcare Administration from Wilmington University in Delaware.

Currently, Kanla excels as a Human Resource Data Specialist at the University of Delaware, providing analytical support to numerous departments, notably the Engineering Department. Beyond her role at the university, she is passionate about financial literacy and empowers families to achieve financial independence as a Financial Literacy Education Professional with World Financial Group. Kanla also serves as a brand ambassador for ONPASSIVE, a cutting-edge AI IT software company.

**Sarah Craster** is a high school teacher of English as an Additional Language and English Language Arts. She has been teaching at least one of those two subjects at the high school level since 2017. In 2013, while pursuing her master's degree in Teaching English as a Second Language, she met Matanda at the University of Delaware's Banned Books readout.

For her undergraduate degree, Sarah majored in English with two minors in Linguistics and Spanish. She has a passion for literacy, language, and literature, as well as equity in education. As a former student of English, she is also passionate about reading or viewing speculative fiction (science fiction and fantasy), telling stories through both words and music, and being dramatic.

**Christina M. Lisk** is committed to disability advocacy in the non-profit sector and the arts. She has publications in various channels, including *The Mighty*, *Yahoo Finance*, and Hearinglikeme.com and a short story in *Nothing Ever Happens in Fox Hollow Anthology: Vol 2*. Her disability love story is a novel in progress, which, in 2019, she presented at Middlebury Bread Loaf in Sicily. Outside of this, Christina epitomizes, "I'm going to die petting something I shouldn't," referring to dogs and cats that overfill her phone and where she pets and sits, no matter where.

**Ambrosia Kweh-Mondoa** is an author and educator of intercultural development and a community advocate. She holds a PhD in education and human development from Michigan State University, a Master's in Educational Counseling from Wilmington University, and a Bachelor's in Education from the University of Delaware. She has over forty years of professional experience in the field of education and educational counseling. She has presented and held African cultural events for over ten years in the state of Delaware. These events provided an opportunity for professionals to participate and share their knowledge, experience, and expertise in their respective fields.

For the past eight years, Ambrosia has visited Cameroon yearly, and each time, she takes her American friends to experience the Cameroonian culture. She worked for the People to People Student Ambassador Program, founded by US President Dwight Eisenhower, where she took students to different countries in Europe, South America, and Oceania to experience different cultures. She presented at a Women's Studies Symposium at Oxford University, where she spoke on gender roles and using the dividend created by artificial intelligence to compensate childcare and elder care workers.

She lives in Delaware with her husband, a neonatal doctor, and cherishes international travel, reading, and gardening. She is the author of *Go, Tell Michelle* and *The Power of Connecting with People*.

## ABOUT THE PUBLISHER

Spears Books is an independent publisher dedicated to providing innovative publication strategies with emphasis on Africana stories and perspectives. As a platform for alternative voices, we prioritize the accessibility and affordability of our titles to ensure that relevant and often marginal voices are represented in the global marketplace of ideas. Our titles – poetry, fiction, narrative nonfiction, memoirs, reference, travel writing, African languages, and young people's literature – aim to bring African worldviews closer to diverse readers. Our titles are distributed in paperback and electronic formats globally by African Books Collective.

**Connect with Us:** Go to www.spearsbooks.org to learn about exclusive previews and read excerpts of new books, find detailed information on our titles, authors, subject area books, and special discounts.

**Subscribe to our Free Newsletter:** Be amongst the first to hear about our newest publications, special discount offers, news about bestsellers, author interviews, coupons and more! Subscribe to our newsletter by visiting www.spearsbooks.org

**Quantity Discounts:** Spears Books are available at quantity discounts for orders of ten or more copies. Contact Spears Books at orders@spearsmedia.com.

**Host a Reading Group:** Learn more about how to host a reading group on our website at www.spearsbooks.org